ONE COIN FOUND

ONE COIN FOUND

How God's Love Stretches to the Margins

EMMY KEGLER

Fortress Press

Minneapolis

ONE COIN FOUND
How God's Love Stretches to the Margins

Cover design: Paul Soupiset

Print ISBN: 978-1-5064-4821-3
eBook ISBN: 978-1-5064-4829-9

The paper used in this publication meets the minimum requirements of American National Standard for Information Sciences—Permanence of Paper for Printed Library Materials, ANSI Z329.48-1984.

Manufactured in the U.S.A.

To my mother,
who first heard my stories and gave me my voice.

To my beloved Michelle:
every next chapter of my life has you in it.

TABLE OF CONTENTS

FOREWORD

Emmy Kegler is the best kind of weird.

She is a Lutheran pastor with an impressive command of Scripture and a passion for innovative worship; she considers doodling one of her spiritual gifts. Her boardgame nights are legendary, and her one-of-a-kind cackle will set even the staunchest wallflower at ease. Emmy recently led a sermon series on the animals of the Bible, drawing insights from everything from the chicken of Matthew 23 to the beast of Revelation 13. She created a database for cross-referencing her friends' Enneagram numbers, zodiac signs, Hogwarts houses, and Myers-Briggs types, "just for fun," and made a protest shirt to wear with her clergy collar that reads, "My Boss Sent Me." This book includes 111 endnotes and six pages of suggested further reading . . . and it's a *memoir*.

But what I love most about Emmy is her fierce, unrelenting love for her fellow oddballs—for religious burnouts and political misfits, for queer Christians seeking refuge and healing from toxic faith environments, for doubters and dreamers and wilderness wanderers, for recovering know-it-alls like me.

Hers is a church that colors outside the lines, a church full of what she calls "the impossibilities of God." And indeed, as her own impossible journey unfolds in the pages before you, it becomes clear that Emmy understands better than most what the disciple Philip knew when he baptized the Ethiopian eunuch on the wilderness road to Gaza that day: that the Spirit moves in the margins, that ours is a God who meets us in "the stories of impossibility, of water in the desert and food in time of drought."

This book is water in the desert, a table of fresh food in the wilderness. It nourished me in ways I didn't expect, inviting this lifelong church nerd to see stories from the Bible in fresh, startling ways. With tenderness and skill, Emmy weaves the strands of her own story into the grander story of God's relentless love for the world, but in a way that is never preachy and never self-satisfied. I've been grateful for Emmy's work for many years now, but as I turned the pages of this beautiful memoir, I found myself grateful too for the ragamuffin souls who helped her along the way—the mother who loved her unconditionally, the liberation theologians who gave language to her experience, the eccentric bearded pastor who plopped a plate of communion bread in her hands and said, "There you go. You've been trained."

To think of all the impossible stories that led to this one being told!

Of course, the impossible story at the center of this book is the story of the lost coin, but I'll let Emmy tell that one; she does it more justice. I'm just here to encourage you to read on, to remind you to savor, to urge you to slow down and *pay attention* because every last one of these hard-won words is for *you*—

you, who are immeasurably beloved by God,

you, who know a thing or two about coloring outside the lines,

you, who, with the help of the great communion of saints, can embrace all the best kinds of weird,

you, who will always and ever be found.

Rachel Held Evans
author of *Searching for Sunday* and *Inspired*

PROLOGUE

Lost

I want to tell you, beloved, about the lost chapter of the Bible. You've probably already found it. It's one of those secrets hiding in plain sight. You might know the feeling—like everyone who meets you sees you, but doesn't really see you. You feel like you're giving every possible signal other than tattooing it on your forehead, but still others don't recognize you for who you are.

I want to tell you about the lost chapter of the Bible, the one with the story of a shepherd who leaves ninety-nine sheep behind and goes out looking for the one that is lost. The one with the story of a woman who sweeps her entire house looking for the one coin that is lost. The one with the lost son who wanders from home and a lost son who stays and stews in his resentment and a lost father struggling to reunite his broken family.[1]

This isn't a lost story. This is our story.

We know this story, don't we? Especially that prodigal son. Those of us who have walked away from abusive homes and abusive churches, who have turned our backs on the places that turned their backs on us—we know this story, because in every casting call we get the role of the younger son. The greedy one, the squanderer of wealth, the one who walks away from everything good to live among swine just so he could have his way. We've been told that's us. My queer family knows this story all too well. When we name our sexuality or our gender identity, or when our friends and family claim us as beloved, we hear this story. We've been told, so many of us in so many ways, that we're just like that son, turning our back on everything good because we want to have the world our way.

But I've come to wonder if the other two stories in this lost chapter of the Bible can tell us a little more about our own lost selves.

If the analogy holds, if we're the lost second son, we're also the lost sheep. We went wandering. We put the whole herd in danger, you know, because we followed our stubborn sheep nose and the shepherd had to leave the ninety-nine and chase us down.

You know what's funny about sheep? They wander. That's what they do; it's in their nature. Most herd animals do it. That's why, when humans domesticated cattle and goats and yes, sheep, there arose a new role: the shepherd, the rancher, the cowboy. Someone's got to keep the herd together, because otherwise they'll go wandering off. It isn't some rebellion against intrinsic sheep-ness; it's not malicious or sinful or particularly stubborn, really. Sheep wander. It's what they do.

And sheep wander for good reasons. They wander because they're hungry. The shepherd didn't bring them to a fertile enough field, and they're fighting with each other for good grass or sweet water. And these are desert sheep, mind you, wandering through the Middle Eastern wilderness—there isn't always a lot of green to go around. If the shepherd isn't careful, the sheep end up starving.

Sometimes the sheep are sick, or injured, or old. They're exhausted from the heat or tired from the walk. They drop to the back of the herd, lie down somewhere to rest. If the shepherd isn't watching for those on the edges, the group might move on without them. You've got to have a good shepherd, someone who's watching for the sheep that are hurting.

And sometimes sheep run. A hundred sheep are a hundred potential meals for the wolves that wander that same wilderness. Especially a sheep that's already not paying attention, already trying to find better food or get some rest to regain their strength—that sheep is easy pickings for the predator. So the sheep run, fleeing as fast as their hooves can take them, getting them lost but keeping them alive. If you don't have a shepherd watching for the wolves, the sheep can end up missing—or a meal.

We've all known shepherds like that. Shepherds unable to see that we're hungry or hurting or hounded by wolves that seek to tear us apart. Leaders and friends who, through passive or active indifference, see our hunger and our hurts and write them off as inconsequential. We've known this too well. We have hungers and hurts that people who have not struggled as we have can't imagine. And so, we go wandering. We try to find something that will feed us, somewhere safe to rest, someone to protect us from a world that wants to devour us.

And if the analogy holds, if we are the second son and the lost sheep, we too are the lost coin. A manmade symbol of worth and value, part of a decorative collection or simply the money needed to buy that day's bread. We're that lost coin, precious and yet hidden, rolled under a cabinet or hidden in an unswept bit of dust.

The funny thing about coins is that they can't get lost by themselves. They can't roll away on their own. Coins get lost because their owners aren't careful; whoever was in charge was wasteful with them. Coins get lost because they lose their shine, because dirt and rust cling to them, and without careful attention, they turn a color indistinguishable from dust and mess. Some of us know that story of the golden Buddha—a solid gold statue hidden under layers of mud, meant to protect a monastery's treasure from marauding armies. Sometimes I think of the lost coin that way, a shiny penny so covered in years of grit that it falls easily to the floor of a car or the sand of a sidewalk, dropped and forgotten.

We've known leaders like that, too. There were leaders who saw our value as something to be squandered, something they could be careless with. They saw the beauty of our bodies as something to be used, but our wounds and trauma as something to be whitewashed over. They saw our hope and devotion as a way to build their own platform, but our questions and concerns as something to be shoved aside. They saw the richness of racial diversity as a way to prove their own skill but refused to face the systems that perpetuated division and oppression. And for nearly every member of my queer family, there were friends who watched without interfering when accusations of abomination and sinfulness battered us until our shine was hidden beneath layers of other people's hatred.

The trouble with this metaphor is that God is the shepherd and the woman, and if God was careless with sheep and coin that would mean God was careless with us. Metaphors, in Scripture and elsewhere, do not encompass the whole of reality. God has never been careless with us, but those who claim to speak for God have. We experience God through our experiences of others. We experience God through the Scripture handed down to us over centuries, translated and retranslated, edited and sweated over. We experience God through how others use those same Scriptures, supporting both slavery and abolition, egalitarianism and complementarianism. We experience God through compassionately curated events, from regular Sunday worship to Wednesday-night Bible studies to weekend retreats, and all the experiences of God that our leaders have had create filters for our own experiences. And too often—because really, even once is too often—those leaders look at us, we precious hungry sheep and dusty dropped coins, the very things that God-as-shepherd and God-as-woman is straining with all her might to keep safe, and they don't see us in our beautiful bodies as made in the image of God. They don't see the dappled diversity of our skin as a gift but as a task to be completed, a mix to be separated. They don't see the gentleness of our love, how it makes us more ready to care for others and do God's work in the world.

Those leaders look at us and only see a sinful second son.

The prodigal son. That's the name we gave him. Prodigal: lavish, reckless, extravagant. Spending money he shouldn't. He takes his inheritance and takes off, squanders it, lives recklessly, then comes home with his tail between his legs.

But just as with the sheep and the coin, if the metaphor holds, then I as the second son have some questions.

What is so broken in this family that the second son leaves? To say to a father "I want my inheritance now" is to say "I wish you were dead." How has this family fractured so badly? Is that second son, like hungry sheep, not fed well enough, not cared for? Is he, like a coin without its luster, forgotten in the shine of the dutiful older brother? Is the blame for his leaving all with him, or, like the shepherd and the woman, does the father too bear responsibility?

I as the second son, the wasteful, the sinner, have a question: Why does the father give him the money? Is it resignation, an acceptance that his sinful son has turned too far against him to turn back? Is it given with a sneer, a frustrated toss of a coin bag: *Fine, go, if you think you can do better on your own!*

I wonder, as that second son who has had to turn her back on places that wounded her, if the father had regrets. If he wished he'd done something differently: not given the money, paid more attention, gone after the son and stood in the road and begged him to return. But he doesn't. He gives the son the money, and he lets him go.

And I have a question, as a woman and a daughter: where is the mother? Where is the societal glue that would have held this first-century family together? If she is alive, why does she not grab father and son both by the ear until they work their quarrel out without such a traumatic break first? Or is she dead and cannot advocate for the lesser of the sons, cannot find a way to make peace where there are three men in pain?

I as the second son, the wasteful, the sinner, have a question: why is the father willing to welcome him home without an apology? The son's practiced speech, whether sincere or contrived, is interrupted not with condemnation or passivity but a cry for servants to bring a ring and shoes and a robe— the best robe. This is some welcome for a grand sinner. Perhaps just coming home was enough of an apology. Perhaps just coming home was enough.

The father didn't go looking for him, but he saw him from a long way off. I like that image, the father pacing the edge of his land, wrinkled hand shielding aging eyes, peering off into the distance where he last saw his second son. He didn't go after him, but he didn't stop looking for him. Maybe there was transformation for the father, too. Maybe while the son misspent his money, the father was regretting misspending his time. Maybe when his son was hungry for rotting pods, the father was hungry for reconciliation. Maybe, if something was wrong enough in the family to make the son leave, there was something right enough in the leaving to make the father change.

What I think, my fellow second sons, is that we were told the truth. This story is for us. We are the prodigal son. But too we are lost and hungry sheep. We have gone unfed, walked without rest, been chased by wolves, and our friends and leaders did not see our pain. But God, in big and little ways, has donned a shepherd's cloak and come running after us. God, in big and little ways, has clambered over rocks and climbed down cliffs. God has found us, hungrier and more hurt and terrified, and cradled us close to say: *No matter why you left or where you went, you are mine.*

We too are lost and dusty coins. We have gone unnoticed, rusted from others' indifference, misspent and misused, and our friends and leaders did not see our neglect. But God, in big and little ways, has picked up a woman's broom and swept every corner of creation. God, in big and little ways, has tucked up her skirts and flattened herself on the floor, dug through dust bunnies and checked every dress pocket. God has found us, dustier and rustier and without any luster, and held us up to the light to say: *No matter how you rolled away or what corner you were dropped in, you are mine.*

We have been unwanted, rejected, sent away with anger or with sadness at our rebellious streak. We have seen both glory and starvation, both beauty and pig pens, and we are coming home footsore and heartbroken. And before the words are out of our mouth, before our perfect speech is performed, God is cloaking our dirty shoulders in the best robe, slipping a ruby ring on our work-worn fingers, cleaning off the pig slobber to slip sandals on our feet, and declaring: *I am so sorry you had to go, and I am eternally glad to have you back again.*

These stories, beloved, are for us too.

CHAPTER 1

Fairy tales are more than true: not because they tell us that dragons exist, but because they tell us that dragons can be beaten.

—Neil Gaiman

"Emmy, do you think God is a boy?"

I was three. My mother was driving me home from a friend's birthday party at the local pizza place. Sneakers swinging, I was buckled into the booster chair, contentedly playing with my parting gift—a balloon animal. It was an indistinct blob with wings, and I was flying it through the air, babbling to myself in a singsong tone: "Our father whoart in heaven, hallow'd bee thy name . . ."

Mom glanced in the rearview mirror, trying to catch my eye. I played on without notice. We had been reciting the Lord's Prayer before bed each night, but Mom was wrestling with the decision; she had been reading a number of books and was not certain about giving me language for speaking about the divine that cast God as male.

"Emmy, do you think God is a boy? Or could God be a girl?"

I answered, quite matter-of-factly and without pause: "*Mom*. God is like my balloon animal." I turned it in my hand, showing off the rounded wings, nearly translucent with air. "If you turn it this way, it looks like a butterfly." I spun it the other way and flew it through the air again. "If you turn it that way, it looks like a bee."

My mother turned back to look at me. I was, so the story goes, unperturbed; I had said my piece. When we got home, she sat my father down and said: *We need to get this kid in a church.*

She was not worried about the state of my soul. Mom had left organized religion years before, unsatisfied by rigid doctrine that rejected birth control and had aligned itself with a right-wing government perpetrating atrocities in Vietnam. She'd also found less and less loving kindness in the church and could not reconcile how so many associated with it, particularly the rigid teachers from her Catholic school, could be following the ways of Christ. The church, at least in my mother's eyes, was not going to save me. It was, however, going to save my parents from being solely responsible for whatever natural spiritual inclinations I already had.

Both my parents, twenty-three years apart, had grown up in Catholic families, with several years of Catholic school education. My mother alternately told stories of nuns who were generous and compassionate, scathing and demanding. My father's brother, Maynard, had been ordained into the Oblate of Mary Immaculate in his early twenties; at sixty-one, Uncle Maynard had baptized me at the church of Saint Walburga. Not yet five months old, I screamed through the whole Mass, start to finish. This was, perhaps, a less than auspicious beginning to my relationship with the church.

Although I was baptized Catholic, neither of my parents was practicing. Mom had left the church in the mid-seventies; Dad, even earlier, moving into a Lutheran congregation for his first wife. Together they decided to raise me in the church; Dad wanted to return to Catholicism, Mom was willing to try. They started Catholic reentry classes, trying two different local parishes, but at both, my mother was hit with the same rejection that had characterized her earlier life in the church. She sat my father down again: "I'm not going back to the Catholic Church." They stopped searching for a while, until the day of the balloon animal, and my mother looked at my father after dinner and said: "I can't raise my daughter somewhere that tells her she can't do something because she's a girl. What if someday she wants to become a priest?"

My father smiled. "What are the odds of *that* happening?"

So we became Episcopal—a common place for post-Catholic families, with the high-church liturgical practices of the Roman tradition but the progressive theology of the main-line. Mom invested in books like *To Dance with God* and began to integrate the rhythm of our family life with the liturgical year. We decorated the whole house on December 5 every year in preparation for St. Nicholas Day. A toy nativity was put in my hands, and I was encouraged to tell and retell and re-retell the story of Jesus's birth. We attended the full cycle of Holy Week services—Maundy Thursday, Good Friday, Holy Satur-day. There was a distinct pattern to our life as a family, the cycle of seasons matched with a cycle of religious story. Life had a purpose and a season and a rhythm to it.

From my earliest days, my mother loved me fiercely and unconditionally. Mom was determined to give me the mother she had never had; her own mother had been highly anxious and often contentious and had died of complications from breast cancer when my mother was a teenager. Mom commit-ted herself to "raising me right," studying modern parenting books about clear communication, paying careful attention to the VHSes that slowly invaded the house, surrounding me with books and reading to me at night. She provided a secure and engaging environment in which I could explore and grow.

Mom grounded me in family stories. A first-generation Italian in the middle of the little Scandinavia that is Minne-sota, she knew what it was like to be an outsider. In particular she told me stories of Great-Great-Uncle Angelo, who worked in the granite quarries of Wilmington, Delaware. He was so strong he could crack a boulder as tall as himself in half with a single hammer blow. When the family transitioned from quarry into factory work, Angelo went with them. In America, each immigrant group from Europe suffered under the poor treatment of those who had made it before them, and my mother's family was no exception; the grown children of Irish and Scottish immigrants, more integrated and longer employed, were antagonized by the arrival of Italian immigrants to the factory. My great-grandfather and his brothers were able to save up and buy a car to drive to work—an early Model A—and their coworkers, enraged by the audacity, parked their own cars bumper-to-bumper with it, hemming it in in front and in back. No amount of slow inching forward or back (which the Model A was not particularly capable of doing) would free it. My ancestors stood outside with hands balled into fists while their rivals stood inside laughing.

Great-Great-Uncle Angelo, so the story goes, bent down and wedged his fingers into the bright white spokes of the Model A's front tires. Little by little, inch by inch, he tugged the car sideways, front then back, front then back. (It weighed over two thousand pounds.) The car was pulled free, and—so the story goes—the other immigrant families never bothered our family again.

These were the stories that fed me, sitting around the kitchen table or curled into my mother's lap in front of the fireplace. *We come from a strong people, clever and self-sufficient, able to overcome the obstacles others lay before us.* Mom raised me to be capable with both housework and home repair. I excelled in school and was continually praised by my teachers. I learned that I, too, was clever and capable, and from there

I developed an independent streak: I liked to be self-reliant, even at a young age, and I often turned down the assistance of others, even when I needed it, out of a thirst to prove myself. I lived also with the solitariness of an only child; I learned to be alone and to cultivate a life of the mind. My natural introversion was uninterrupted by siblings. I had an active imagination, creative impulses, and a hunger for books.

My voracious literary appetite, unlike my spiritual inclinations, caught no one by surprise. Both my parents were English teachers; my father going on to be a university professor, and my mother, a community college instructor. The house was stocked with books: poetry collections, historical accounts of World War II, grammatical analyses, essays by Annie Dillard. One of my most prized possessions was (and remains) a signed copy of *The New Beacon Book of Quotations by Women*. Even before I could read, if I woke during the night, I would pull picture book after picture book into bed with me, leafing through the pages and gazing at the pictures until I fell asleep again, to wake in the morning surrounded by half-open copies of Dr. Seuss's *Horton Hatches the Egg* and Shel Silverstein's *The Missing Piece*. Children's books, above all else, tell such glorious stories, the words carefully crafted for rhythm and clarity, the tales wrapped in gorgeous illustrations. Like the rhythm of my home life, the stories of books held meaning; they had narrative and trajectory, offered opportunities for self-reflection and transformation, and always promised resolution by the final page. They were as real and true as the family stories that told me who I had come from; my storybooks told me who others had been and offered me, too, the chance to determine my own destiny, to trust in my instincts and gifts.

Books supplied me with models for capable, self-sufficient, creative, and stubborn young girls—girls, I felt, who were just like me. I didn't have an older sister to lead the way. I had Laura Ingalls and Caddie Woodlawn, pioneer girls, whose stories of surviving droughts and dealing with one-room-schoolhouse bullies reminded me that I, too, had the strength and resourcefulness to make it through anything. Felicity Merriman promised me that my scraped knees and pocket-knife mishaps (when Mom says don't climb a tree with an open blade there is a *good reason*) didn't make me any less of a girl, and I could be just as much myself in a pretty dress at a fancy ball as I could sneaking out to ride my cruel neighbor's skittish horse and brush her coat until she shone, both inside and out, like a pretty penny. I was actually afraid of horses as a child, but the abstract concept applied—grown-ups might be bitter and callous, but I knew better, and if I could get around them long enough, I'd prove them wrong.

Annemarie Johansen taught me what it was like to be a Christian during the second World War, with my Jewish neighbors constantly under threat of being taken away during the night. From her I learned that there was nothing that should come between me and what was right—not fear, not bodily harm, not even the truth. If the truth was that my supposed sister was actually my Jewish best friend hiding in plain sight in my house because her parents couldn't get her out, and the Nazis asked me who she was, then the truth was *she was my sister*. (Later in life when I was introduced to Kant's categorical imperative, and its critiques, I was unimpressed. I had long known truth was subject to reality.)

Books, and their heroines, also opened up magical worlds. In the era just before Hermione Granger, it was Lucy Pevensie and Meg Murry who walked beside me through the dark. It was their differences—Lucy's wide-eyed embrace of a new world and Meg's stubborn anger and protective love—that made them special; their weirdness allowed them to conquer whatever came before them, not because they were more powerful than it but because they could see beyond the powers of evil and, instead, grip onto a power for good.

From historical fiction came historical biography. Anne Hutchinson taught me to stand up for what I believed in, despite the scowls of the Puritan men of the Massachusetts Bay Colony. Elizabeth Blackwell showed me how to apply for a school that should never take me and be too brilliant to be denied. Nellie Bly raced around the world, unafraid of what could happen to a young unmarried woman daring to ride in hot-air balloons. And Harriet Beecher Stowe, of course, reminded me of the power that a well-crafted story carries—sometimes strong enough to shake the ethics of a country divided over racial chattel slavery. From the beginning, I learned a crucial lesson: stories did not have to be true to be real.

My love for story, however, did not prepare me for the world of Scripture. I came to the Bible in a deeply liturgical setting, surrounded by light filtered through colored glass and spilling over dark pews. The altar was covered in tall candle-sticks, the flickering flames reflecting in the gilded curves of the metal around them. The choir and acolytes wore robes, with blue button-up cassocks under a crisp white surplice, shining dress shoes lightly scuffed on the toes from when we knelt for prayer. The ceiling arched four stories into the sky, where sermon words and organ chords echoed transcenden-tally, enveloping the congregation in the sounds.

And, oh, the music—the music! Between the choir and the organ and the full-throated voices of the congregation, it was inescapable. I followed along in our hymnal, my fin-ger tracing words to stories I was coming to learn: *O come o come Emmanuel, and ransom captive Israel.* When crocuses bloomed and trees began to bud, we swayed with lullabies: *Fair are the meadows, fair are the woodlands, rob'd in flow'rs of blooming spring.* As spring crested into summer, we pro-claimed our confidence in God's power: *Immortal, invisible, God only wise! In light inaccessible, hid from our eyes!* Around and around the seasons went, wrapped in fervent prayers: *Almighty God, to you all hearts are open, all desires known, and from you no secrets are hid: cleanse the thoughts of our hearts by the inspiration of your Holy Spirit, that we may perfectly love you, and worthily magnify your holy Name.* Each Sunday the adults received the Eucharist, the promise of the presence of God wrapped up with the promise of our own possibilities: *Sanctify them by your Holy Spirit to be for your people the Body and Blood of your Son, the holy food and drink of new and unending life in him. Sanctify us also that we may faithfully receive this holy*

Sacrament, and serve you in unity, constancy, and peace. Words had power, I learned.

The stories came alive elsewhere too. In Sunday school, we were carefully guided through the stories of the faith and the teachings of Jesus, carefully pouring colored melted wax to make our very own "let your light shine" candle or watching a butterfly emerge from a chrysalis to learn about what death and resurrection look like. My teachers (all women) were generous with glue sticks and glitter, tenderhearted with us and gentle in their lesson planning, ushering our little classrooms of ten or twelve through the story and the questions and the craft with a mother's expansive love.

This was how I came to know the stories of God: wrapped in color and light, sound and song, tenderness and patience, rhythm and ritual. But Scripture was not just for Sundays; the stories came home with us. My mother invested in picture Bibles and single-issue storybooks that told me the tales of heroines in the faith. Hannah was confident in her faith, rejected a powerful priest's understanding of her tears, and praised God with celebration: *My heart exults in the Lord, my strength is exalted in the Lord. God raises up the poor from the dust, the needy from the ash heap, and makes for them a seat of honor.* Mary Magdalene, possessed by seven demons that made her scream and shout, was freed by the man Jesus of Nazareth and followed him, even unto death, and because of her courage and loyalty was the first to see him when he rose.[1]

And Deborah—my favorite—rose up to teach the people of Israel, to sit under her palm and decide their verdicts, and she raised up Barak against the evil iron-charioted Sisera and freed the people from their oppression under the terrible King Jabin.[2] Sisera escaped the battle, and Jael pretended she would protect him—but knowing what a cruel man he was, she waited until he slept and then drove a tent peg through his skull. (It should be noted that not every Bible story is appropriate for young children.) I loved the story of Deborah and Jael, two underestimated women, getting serious comeuppance on a brutal regime. This is the Scripture I learned first—stories of strong women who served a God like my mother, tender and caring and unafraid to fight for her children.

I would eventually find out this was not how everyone else viewed God. First, everyone else seemed to think that God was male. This was confusing, since at creation we'd all been made in the image of God *and* as far as I could tell, God was supposed to be everywhere, and although men were trying, they had not yet accomplished universal omnipresence. God didn't have a body. Okay, there was the one time, but other than that, God was transcendent. Clearly I was going to have to take this faith thing into my own hands, since the adults were not clever enough to have figured it out.

The more I read my third-grade copy of *The Good News*, the more holes I found in what the adults were handing down. There were only two Christmas accounts, and they differed significantly. Who received the annunciation, Joseph or Mary? Did Jesus live in Bethlehem or had they traveled there for a census? Did the wise men find him in a house under a star or did the shepherds find him in an inn wrapped in swaddling

clothes?[3] The single story that I'd come to know from pag-
eants and recited over my wooden toy nativity was two stories,
mashed together, and poorly so. My minor crisis of faith didn't
even account for how the little lord Jesus probably cried, no
matter what the song said. It wasn't so much that I was mad
that the story wasn't real; it was that no one had told me. Why
would anyone tell the same story over and over and not mention it was *two*?

This was the danger and the blessing of my liberal main-
line upbringing: I was not raised to be afraid of God. I was
not taught to be too scared to question. All of my models
for living, from my mother to my storybook heroines to the
faithful women of the Scriptures, told the same story: we are
a people who push back. We do not accept the status quo.
We do not assume that those in power were granted their
privilege by divine right but by human systems. We refuse to
accept cruelty as the end-all. We fight back. We find what is
real beneath the truth.

And so, when my high-school humanities teacher introduced creation myths and showed us that there were two—
two—creation stories in the Bible, and one of them was wet
and one of them was dry and both of them conformed to
other types of creation myths throughout ancient civiliza-
tions,[4] I was not overly shocked. When my college professor
assigned Borg's *Meeting Jesus Again for the First Time*, and we
as a class began to unweave the four strands of Gospel narratives and compare the synoptics against each other,[5] I was not

astounded for long. Each time I encountered it, the idea that the Bible was fallible was only momentarily startling. Of course it was. It was a story. All the stories I'd ever known were just that—stories. Annemarie never existed to save her best friend Ellen from the Nazis. There was no Aslan and no wardrobe to Narnia (though I would, later, find a different kind of closet door to open up a whole new world). Laura Ingalls Wilder probably didn't do half the things she claimed she did, and her books perpetuated horrific and racist stereotypes of indigenous American people. Stories weren't meant to be infallible. The narrative arc was limited, and the events were molded to fit the theme. They weren't true, not in an exact scientific or historical sense. They were stories, and they were real.

So were the tales of Babel and of the Reed Sea. So were the legends of Samson and Elijah. So was the poetry of the psalms and the love song of Solomon; so were the prophecies of Isaiah and the visions of Revelation.[6] So were the books of Samuel and Kings and Chronicles, who couldn't quite seem to get their facts straight. So was the fiery furnace of Daniel and the flash of light on Paul's road to Damascus.[7] They were stories—they didn't have to be true. All I needed was for them to be real.

I needed them to tell me who my ancestors had been and what had mattered to them so I might know where I had come from and what had been passed down into my care. I needed to know who the heroines were, so I might have models of courage and compassion. I needed a theme, an overarching narrative, a direction in which the story was going, a promise that the ending—no matter how seemingly impossible—would be a good one. I didn't need the Scriptures to be infallible or to be the word of God; they themselves confessed they were not. They were a testimony to the Word, who became flesh and lived among us.[8]

The stories weren't meant to be infallible. But that didn't make them any less real.

CHAPTER 2

Mom woke me at 3:00 a.m. I dressed sleepily, my eyelids still weighty, pulling on jeans and a shirt in the strange stillness of early morning dark. We drove to church mostly in silence. I was tempted to lie down across the cracked leather backseat of the Buick and go back to sleep. But not sleeping was the whole point.

We arrived at church and found the old and heavy sanctuary door unlocked. As we slipped inside, the first thing that struck me was the change in the air. Outside was cool and damp, the start of a spring dew, the moonlight speckling over new buds on the trees. Inside was a golden darkness, the dark-stained wood lit by candle after candle, and the air was heavy with the scent of flowers—like a weighted blanket turned to atmosphere. The coat room at the back of the sanctuary had been transformed.

The usual hundreds of worn wooden hangers were gone, replaced with wide swaths of burgundy fabric, the shelves on top filled with lilies and hydrangea, white silk bound around their plastic pots. Two dark-stained wood kneelers were placed facing the stained-glass rose window; four chairs, two on each side, created a mini aisle up to them. On one kneeler's book rest was the massive leather-bound Bible, edges gilded and crisp, that usually sat on the pulpit. A hymnal and a prayer book lay on one of the chairs. And all around, the scent of flowers. The narthex was now a space for meditation, where from the close of Maundy Thursday worship to sunrise on Good Friday, hour by hour, someone would keep watch in the garden.

We signed in next to our chosen time, and the previous vigiler smiled and squeezed my shoulder as she left. For an hour, we sat in silence, watching and waiting, as Jesus had begged his disciples to do. I thumbed through the hymnal and the Book of Common Prayer. I read the words of Jesus's last meal again and again. Bread. Wine. Love. Promises. Predictions. Water and towel and bowl. Betrayal and confusion, drunkenness and mourning, sleepiness and sleeplessness, sweat like drops of blood as Jesus prayed: *Father, take this away from me.*[1]

Sometimes I would cry, silently, not understanding why. At age ten, at eleven, at twelve, as that single hour passed again and again in my life, I didn't yet understand why I physically craved that time when the church made space for the burden of suffering, when the liturgical year marked that even God-in-flesh sometimes cannot sleep for weeping. I only knew something in the story resounded in me, a kid becoming a teen, the girl with my grandfather's "million-dollar smile" turning into someone who craved the comfort of being alone.

Most of the church year, as I experienced it, was an exercise in the golden rule—examining and understanding how God in Jesus called us to wisdom and kindness. Sunday morning worship was carefully curated. Seasons passed, marked by gold and red and green and purple, coming back again with a rhythmic promise. Our hymnals were well worn; our prayer books easily fell open to the service of Holy Eucharist, where we confessed the faith and practices of our Episcopal ancestors stretching back over hundreds of years. Sunday school and confirmation lessons were about God's love for us and call to love and care for our neighbor. It was a soothing ritual, not emotionless but an exercise in practiced serenity.

But Holy Week came as a disruption. I relished the shouts of the crowd surrounding Jesus as he marched into Jerusalem, disciples wide-eyed amid the leafy branches around them. The first Palm Sunday was less a ritual procession and more a protest march.[2] *Finally,* the people of God shouted, *finally the Messiah has come!* Finally the violence of Rome would be overthrown, the throne of David taken back. Finally the people of God would be free again, no longer poor and starving in their homeland, under the burden of oppression no more. Even at twelve I understood that cry—the ravenous hunger for freedom, for all the promises of the future to be on the brink of being present. Parents and teachers told me "everyone has a hard time in middle school," "popular kids aren't popular forever," "it gets better." If there had been a march to tear down the in-group–out-group nature of middle school, I would have been first in line to cut pine-tree boughs and lay my winter jacket on the road.

On Holy Monday I stood with the crowd again, my back to the pillared walls, mouth agape, as the heralded son of David threw the temple into an uproar. Sacrificial doves escaped their overturned cages and fled for the skies. Coins of every metal and size, some with the idolatrous head of Caesar stamped upon them, tipped onto the stone floor and rolled in twenty directions. Table after table flipped, and in the midst of it all a searing voice: *The house of prayer made a den of thieves!*[3] I saw the distress on the faces of the disciples, the horror from the priests and scribes, but I felt a strange comfort in Jesus's rage. I knew what it was like to be angry. I knew what it was like to feel anger well up, to try to soothe it down in front of friends and family. Jesus's cleansing of the temple was not a sanctification of anger, his or mine, but it was a promise: anger in and of itself did not make one unholy. Anger in and of itself could be a source for transformation, a reckoning where the most vulnerable had been least cared for. It would take me another twelve years to truly learn to love my own anger, but in this small way my heart was cracked open just enough to breathe in the whisper of possibility that my anger did not make me wretched.

Holy Tuesday, I found, was a mixed bag observance-wise. Jesus launched into several mini-lectures between the cleansing of the temple and the arrival of the Passover, and sometimes we tried to cram them all into one service.[4] I relished the rich foolishness of it, of Jesus's desperate attempts to explain his work to the religious elite, of the continual failure of those who should know best. I was coming of age in the era of Westboro Baptist's rise to fame. It was not hard to see the parallels between the blind guides and hypocrites Jesus condemned, and those who neglected justice and mercy and faith today. As I grew older I would learn of the way the Western church had used Jesus's condemnations as fuel for anti-Semitism, that Holy Week was a kick-off period for persecution against minority Jewish communities, proclaiming that the ancient cry of "his blood be on us and on our children!"[5] was justification for violence today. The simplistic Greek word for "the Jews" throughout the gospels turned to thick toxin in my mouth. Once upon a time Jesus had wept over Jerusalem; now, perhaps, he wept over us.

Wednesday leaned more heavily into the danger, etched with the story of Judas and all the questions that surround his actions.[6] Was it wasted money, anointing oil that could have been sold and given to the poor? Was it Satan, short and simple, the corrupter of Adam's companion Eve, now indwelt in Jesus's close friend? Preachers questioned his sudden reversal, the disciple turned traitor; how could someone so intimately familiar with Jesus's life and mission find any worth in turning him over to death? How could Judas betray him so easily?

Clearly a question asked by people who have forgotten what middle school is like. Ask any preteen about betrayal and they, too, can tell you of sleepless nights when they sweat blood. Holy Week is a disruption in our shining stained-glass image of Jesus, but it is a disruption that is real and raw for anyone who has known suffering.

It was that disruption I craved. At ten, at eleven, at twelve, something was going wrong inside me. I would start fights with boys over inconsequential remarks, my fists and feet swinging wildly. Most days at recess I'd sit alone on the empty baseball bleachers, crying quietly into the sleeves of my winter jacket so my face wouldn't freeze. I couldn't seem to make and keep friends. My grades were good, but I was often uncooperative, challenging teachers on assignments that I found too narrow and refusing to compromise with my peers in group work.

I also got caught writing anonymous love notes. I'd used my left hand and a forgotten red pen to scrawl four-line rhyming poems to every girl in class, never signing any name, slipping them into their desks when we left for gym. I didn't know why, exactly. I only knew that they were sad, that they were starting, at age ten and eleven, to talk about how they were fat and ugly, and I wanted them to feel beautiful and admired. One of them caught me, because it's not that hard to catch someone hiding under their hardtop desk and using their nondominant hand. I'd already struggled to get along with the other girls in my class, always feeling left out for reasons I couldn't identify. Now I had marked myself as "weird," and the isolation expanded.

I wasn't a problem kid. I didn't have divorced parents or not enough lunch money. Mom was home when I got off the bus; Dad was there to drive me to T-ball. Adult after adult tried to identify what was making me so volatile and withdrawn. I was bounced from solution to solution, my parents and teachers certain they could find an explanation for why a bright student with well-off and attentive parents was alternately aggressive, weepy, and reclusive. One year it was behavioral management, in a wall-carpeted room where we problem kids would turn six-sided pillows around in our laps until our Feelings Cube accurately reflected, from the available options, our emotion at that moment. The next year it was the Gifted and Talented program, with messy physics experiments and a host of musical instruments we built and played ourselves. The shift barely occurred to me at the time; the behavioral management group had been disbanded (cut from the budget, I assume now) and the Gifted and Talented program had taken over their room. They'd forgotten to take down the Poster of Feelings, though, and there in the bottom left corner, two sketches of two different kids continued to haunt me: one by herself, banging a stick against a fence as she walked home, labeled "Alone"; one sitting in the midst of a busy cafeteria, poking at her PB&J as everyone else leaned a little away from her, marked "Lonely." Those drawings first annoyed me and then haunted me.

I kept trying to find "my people." Mom orchestrated an elaborate birthday party when I turned eleven, with competitive games and point systems and a cabinet of prizes, plus a costume party box, plus ten-minute intervals in the hot tub with Mom leaning out the second-story window to get photos of us all laughing together amid the bubbles. I was slotted into the high-level reading and math groups, excused from fourth grade one day to take statewide assessment tests with the fifth graders. I played T-ball and softball. I started private individual and group therapy with other maladjusted teen girls.

But none of it fit. Something was still disrupted inside me, something yet without a name. In Holy Week I found space made for that disruption. In the yearly ritual of Maundy Thursday, I saw someone like me—surrounded by opportunity, even by family and friends, and yet alone. Over and over he tried to explain himself. "This is my body," he said, and they all looked at each other in puzzlement. "This is the blood of the covenant," he said, and they were probably a little less willing to drink. He tied a towel around his waist and knelt at their feet, the place of a servant and slave, begging them to understand his mission of service, only for Peter to stumble over one assertion after another. "Love one another," he said, over and over again, and they debated who was greatest among them. Year after year I listened, wondered, carefully turned the pages of the gilded Bible to retrace my scriptural steps. Jesus offered metaphor after metaphor to explain who he was, to concretize his mission so that his followers could understand what was to come and carry on after him.

I wondered if he got frustrated. I certainly did. Program after program, therapist after therapist, year after year we tried different labels on me to see what would fit. All of us were seeking the word that could explain who I was, why I was so different. Problem children, gifted, mentally ill—even among misfits I was still a misfit. I tried to push down my sense of isolation, that persistent image of a girl alone in the midst of a crowd. I shopped at the popular stores. I bought jeans at the Gap. I tried to fit in.

When the word finally came, at age fourteen, it was as sudden as a bolt of lightning—illuminating, terrifying, and destructive. No adult suggested it; I found it on my own, like a carving inside a cave I'd not yet wandered far enough into to find. Suddenly my life made sense, and suddenly my life was over. There was no avoiding what the flash of light had shown me, and in the days and months that followed it felt like my self was a tree cut in two. I had no hope for signs of growth amid the wreckage of the storm.

I was gay.

After years of searching for a way to explain myself, I was both relieved and devastated. I knew who I was now, but who I was was so removed from everyone else. No one else was gay. Sure, there were a few notable gay men, but this was two years after Ellen DeGeneres had come out—to widespread recognition and then an almost immediate cancellation of her self-titled sitcom. President Clinton had signed the Defense of Marriage Act the year before that. In the era before instant-access internet news, I'd devoured each newspaper article and *Newsweek* issue, keeping the clippings in a shoebox under my bed. Well before the word *gay* became a label I tried on, I'd been (otherwise inexplicably) fascinated by the national conversations around marriage and identity. Now I kicked that box further underneath my bedframe.

This was not the answer I had wanted. I wanted a way to explain myself to others, a word that would identify why I was different but also make it possible for me to fit in. But where does a gay kid fit in the Midwest in 1999? There was no gay-straight alliance in my middle school; there were no gay *people* that I knew of. Teachers had pink triangles on their door to signify that they were a safe space to talk, but I didn't want to talk, I wanted to *belong*, and I heard what my peers whispered about the unmarried science teacher who kept her hair short. I slipped a question into the anonymous box on my health teacher's desk: *How do I know if I'm gay?* I don't remember her answer; I only remember the laughter of my peers when she read it. In eighth grade, we watched the movie *Philadelphia*, where I learned that being gay meant contracting AIDS from anonymous sex in a porno theater, losing your promising legal career, and then, despite the gorgeousness of your hot-blooded Latino partner, wasting away in a hospital room as your body's immune system destroyed itself. In my supposedly sexually liberal public school education, that was all I ever learned about being gay. I think the Catholic private school kids knew more than I did.

Online, there were only the scrappy beginnings of internet culture, limited mostly to unregulated chatrooms and text-based websites with spinning jpgs and auto-played music. I carefully printed out Gay Teen Q&A lists, staring down at the words over and over: *How do I know if I'm a lesbian?* I didn't need to ask. I knew. I wasn't interested in boys; overall, I found them irritating, a waste of space that could have looked cuter and smelled nicer and not been so aggressive with everything. I craved the attention and affection of other girls. In the midst of others' budding relationships and flirtatious notes stuffed in lockers, when who went to the Friday-night dance with whom was the only worthy topic of conversation on Monday, I knew. I knew I was gay, and I felt I was dead already.

I realized I was gay the year after Matthew Shepard died. I'd saved article after article in that box under my bed, piecing together the brutal story of a college kid pistol-whipped until he was covered in blood, tied to a fence along a remote road, and left to die. I didn't need to look far for those who claimed that Matthew had brought his death upon himself. At one point, one of his own murderers said they'd only planned to rob him but then became violent when Matthew made an advance on him. Westboro Baptist was the best-known but not the only anti-gay Christian group to protest his funeral and picket outside the trials of his killers. At thirteen, I shut out the connections between my own faith and the religion that spurred people to cheer the brutal death of a twenty-one-year-old. People like that lived in Alabama or Arizona or Wyoming. They didn't live in Minnesota. People who believed that gays deserved their own slaughter didn't live in my neighborhood. People who gnashed their teeth against Ellen and Matthew and Brandon Teena and every other person who dared to be honest about themselves weren't anyone I'd ever know. This was the lie I had to tell myself when I was thirteen; this was the lie that began to come undone when I was fourteen. I was beginning to understand that my interest in this thing I was learning to call "the LGBT community" was not an academic exercise.

I knew, even then, that as a white lesbian I had a good chance of not dying. AIDS deaths and "gay panic" murders seemed to be limited to gay men and trans people. Somehow this failed to comfort me. I was beginning to understand what the history of gay culture confesses over and over: those with any semblance of power (white, male, cis, educated) might try to escape, but our destiny is tied up together. Matthew and Brandon had died in ways I likely never would, and yet their suffering was bound up in my suffering. In a country enamored with violence, in a world with strictly boundaried ideas of *male* and *female* and *masculine* and *feminine*, in a faith that promised not to take up stones against me but still sought to kill any semblance of my ability to love—my pain was not mine to carry alone, nor were their deaths separate from my own fate.

Perhaps this is why I was fascinated by Jesus's death: I saw the experience of my own people reflected in it. When I was ten years old, our church was host to a traveling Passion Play, a full-scale theatrical reenactment of the final hours of Jesus's life. We saw Jesus torn from his weeping in the garden, hauled from the council of religious elite to Pilate to Herod, mocked and stripped and beaten. As the (fake) blood poured from his back, I crept out of the pew and knelt on the floor, entranced. With every escalating blow of the thirty-nine lashes I crawled forward, pew by pew, until I was crouching by the front-most row, tucking my small body to the side of the aisle in case another band of soldiers came charging down it. I knew it was not real, and yet I had to grip the pew with white-knuckled fingers in order to stop from throwing myself between the lashes and Jesus. In the coming years, every Holy Week, I would play our *Jesus Christ Superstar* LP on repeat and lie on the floor of the carpeted living room, the thuds from the speakers reverberating through my chest. I'd invite friends over to watch the Shroud of Turin documentary, certain they'd be as fascinated as I was with the details of the nail-holes on the wrists and the storied history of a sheet traveling Europe and the Middle East that could supposedly heal the sick. (No one came.)

I was enthralled with the drama of the passion story. Yet I hated the imposition, every Palm Sunday, that in our passion reading the congregation spoke the part of the condemning crowds. Each year I was required to yell *Crucify him! Crucify him!* and sat through sermons that told me how palm-waving praise turned quickly to cries for death. We are a people that love violence, I was reminded. I hated this. My stomach turned each time the crowd's words—*We have no king but Caesar*—were forced into my mouth. Some years I refused to speak it. I knew I was supposed to feel contrite and convicted, to remember that Jesus had died because of my awful sinful nature. But I was developing an allergic resistance to my own condemnation. *Sin* was a broad-reaching category that seemed to encapsulate any instance of falling short of perfection, which made it both universal and commonplace. I bought journals that were supposed to bring me closer to Jesus and further from sin, but they failed to do much more than make me feel even more wretched and alone than I already was. I already knew I wasn't lovable; I was gay. I was probably going to die socially isolated, legally unprotected, and religiously scapegoated. I didn't need to be reminded of it at church.

I wasn't enamored with Jesus's sacrificial death; the drama of the passion, in reality, excluded all that. The cosmic battle between God and Satan for the soul of every created human being resounded with me far less than a man, strikingly different from those around him, offering a message of love, who was turned into a religious and political pawn for the use of others. In the torture and crucifixion of Jesus, I did not see a condemnation. I saw liberation. I saw the truth about what would happen if I chose to live into love. This was my future if I acknowledged who I was and who I would someday love. If I chose to be open about myself, to tell the truth, to proclaim the incredible good news of falling in love with another woman, I would be reviled. Politicians would ignore me until I became enough of a nuisance that they needed to publicly wash their hands of me or, worse, turn me over to state-sanctioned death. Religious leaders would recoil in disgust, would put me on trial on trumped-up charges of heresy, would vomit vitriol at either short self-protective answers or open proclamations of the truth. Friends would betray me, refuse to have known me. One might even turn me in. And at the end of it all, I would be alone in the midday darkness, arms outstretched, hoarse voice crying: *My God, my God, why have you forsaken me?*

This was, in all honesty, good news.

It wasn't good in the sense that it was hopeful. Nor was it good in the sense of "Good Friday because Jesus dying for our sins is Good." It was good because it was true. In the midst of congregational practice that promised acceptance if I volunteered enough, in the midst of a culture that offered safety if I sacrificed myself to my work, I needed honesty. I needed someone to tell me the truth: being gay was not going to be safe. Aligning myself with my newfound family—with gay men who died not of AIDS but of hate, with trans women delegitimized because sex work was the only work they could get, with teens classified as *runaways* because they refused to submit to electroshock therapy, with every woman dying at the end of life unable to legally protect her partner of forty years—was going to destroy me. I would not be able to hide myself, to say as Jesus once had, "tell no one about this."[7] I was going to be required to be honest, to be self-aware, to be ready for a battle with every new person I met. Jesus's slaughter was good because it told the truth about the life to come for me if I accepted being gay.

I needed someone to tell me the truth: pain was real. So real, in fact, that to know what it meant to be human God put on skin and let that body be torn limb from limb. Pain was not escapable; pain was a reality. There was no talisman against it, no behavior that could spare me from it, no confession that could protect me forever. I could not be a good enough Christian or a good enough gay or a good enough anything. I was going to hurt, no matter what, and some of that pain was going to have absolutely nothing to do with whether I was "good enough" or where I'd fallen short. Jesus suffered and died not because he was a sinner but because his full and honest truth made all those in power recoil in fear. Certainly something more cosmic could and would happen in that death, but the story itself bore the truth: Jesus died because the religious and political elite hated him. He died because he intentionally aligned himself with those on the edges. He placed himself among the poor who did not have enough bread for an afternoon on a hillside, among the tax collectors who colluded with the empire, among simple smelly fishermen, among those whose skin puckered with leprous scars or the violence of the demons that possessed them, among women who were Samaritans or bleeding or caught in the act of adultery or foolish enough to sit at his feet and dare to learn. He dared to declare the kingdom of God was at hand and that it was among the last and least. He claimed titles for himself that a carpenter's son from backwater Nazareth had no business speaking: Messiah, Son of Man, Son of God.[8]

I needed this. I needed someone to tell me that all my differences, my impossibilities, my queerness, everything in me that pushed me to the edge of society was not going to prevent my inclusion. I needed to know that all the barriers the world would put up between me and God were worthy of crossing. I needed to hear that no matter how despised and rejected, no matter how acquainted with suffering, no matter how oppressed and afflicted, I was still worth something. The story was that my own sin was the chasm, but what I saw was a culture and a church happy to dig that ditch for me and drop me into it. In Jesus's suffering and death, I heard it declared that no matter what evil and devastation the powers of this world could cook up to silence a message of mercy and love, God was going to find a way to cross it and bring me back.

Of course, no one knew that on the first Friday. There was no goodness in it then. There was only death, the end of all things, the final answer to life's question. The Messiah was gone. God was dead and buried. There was no freedom, no redemption. The God who had split the Reed Sea and brought the chosen people out of slavery did not hear the Son's abandoned cry. "We had hoped he was the one to set Israel free," Cleopas murmured in the dimming light of sunset, on the road to Emmaus.[9]

I grew up in a congregation that celebrated not the Easter Vigil but Holy Saturday. It's an abbreviated version of the Good Friday liturgy, which is likely why few churches do it; it is a truly odd practice to get together *twice* to remember violent death and leave in silence. But for me it spoke more truth. Jesus was in the grave three days. We did not go immediately from Good Friday to Easter morning. There were two long nights in between, one full day of Sabbath when nothing could be done.[10] A full day when all the disciples and the women could do was sit and stare blankly at their dusty floors, their hearts so heavy and broken that a deep breath seemed impossible.

Perhaps they whispered of Judas. Some found themselves vindicated, never having trusted the Iscariot; how well can anyone trust the man who counts the common money? Others whispered of a field called Hakeldama, where Judas met the proper fate of a traitor, and they told their own stories of the righteousness of his death. Surely some were silent, shaken. They had walked beside him, shared meals with him, slept on the same hard floors of whatever generous homeowner had taken them in for the night. Jesus's death had come not from an enemy or an adversary but from a friend, who had walked beside the Teacher in the house of God.[11] Betrayal is not a new story in the life of humanity, but when it appears, it is so wounding as to be silencing.

On the Sabbath, this collection of Jewish followers, the chosen children of God, could not have failed to think of other times of silence. In the shadow of the Passover feast, they now knew intimately the touch of death. In the quiet of unspeakable grief, they remembered Elijah wrapped in his cloak, his face covered, surviving the starvation and the journey and the wind and the earthquake and the fire only to find the Lord in sheer and searing silence. As the Sabbath prayers lifted up the name of the Lord-who-is-One, they remembered the cries of their ancestors in Babylon: *how can we sing the Lord's song in a strange land?*[12]

I try to imagine what it was like to worship in the impossibility of that day. Did they go to the temple or a local synagogue that Sabbath, eyes downcast, feet stumbling with heartsickness? Did the women tug their headscarves closer, unable to meet the eyes of those who had not been there, marked by both grief and shame? Could the women and disciples even go, knowing that it was the religious elite who had united against their Teacher?

I know what it is like to worship among those who have seen your greatest hopes destroyed. I see it in the eyes of my queer and trans family, in their halting steps when they cross a threshold of an unknown sanctuary. We have known. We have known what it's like to leave family behind and pursue a new impossibility. We have fallen in love with something that separates you from all you've known. We have seen the love we gambled on be mocked, beaten, paraded before politicians and pastors only to be condemned and sentenced to execution. We have known the feeling of standing in a crowd, our preachers and teachers with one voice raised against our truth: *Crucify it! Crucify it!*

I would have stayed home that day.

Perhaps they glanced at Simon Peter, his head bowed in his callused hands, and winced with him when the cock crowed that morning of the Sabbath. The men might have counted themselves lucky not to have been caught as Peter had, but there was no denying: all of them had run away, like sheep that scatter when the shepherd is struck.[13] But what else was there to do?

Well, there was what the women did. They watched. They heard his final cries and saw where the body was laid. And they hurried home, for the Sabbath was beginning. But in the midst of their cooking and cleaning, in preparing the fires and candles to last all the night, in dressing the table and wiping their eyes clear to better see what else was needed on that day of preparation, they snuck to the market, or opened their own chests of oils and spices, and made their own preparations for the day to come. This was the story I learned, both in church and in queer life: we go on anyway. In the face of the end we tried to flee but knew was coming, we cook meals for each other and clean under the couch, and we prepare ourselves for the day when we have to bury every hope.

Of course, that's not the end of the story.

CHAPTER 3

MARKED?

Do you want to come to youth group with me sometime?"
Rebecca[1] asked.

Later I would learn to be wary of such invitations. At
sixteen, all I knew was there might finally be a church that
wanted me.

———

My parents raised me in progressive Episcopal congregations
in the suburbs of Saint Paul, Minnesota. I never knew a church
without a woman priest. My calendar year was saturated in
an ancient liturgical cycle: Advent. Christmas. Epiphany. Lent.
Easter. Pentecost. Ordinary Time. And around and around
again, the banners on the pulpit carefully reset and rearranged
each Sunday, the hymns guided along by a persistent and pro-
found organ. In the mainline tradition in which I was raised,

children were often baptized as infants and went through a process of confirmation when they were teens or young adults. Confirmation was our coming-of-age ritual, a yearly event for sixteen-year-olds to read out their Statements of Faith before the congregation, affirm the Nicene Creed, and be recognized by our bishop as full adult members in the church. After that day, we could serve on committees, vote on annual budgets, distribute communion, and—most importantly, at least to me—know that we had spiritually affirmed the covenant our parents had made at baptism.

I started asking to be confirmed at age twelve. Our priest, Father Joe, explained that I had to wait two years until I could begin confirmation classes, and two more after that to actually *be* confirmed. I was furious. I knew what confirmation was all about. I wanted to be recognized as an adult in the church, to claim my faith for myself. This is the curse, I think, of many only children and children of sick parents: I often functioned in my home as a third adult, and I quickly became resentful when my *obvious* maturity was not recognized by outside systems. (I am aware, twenty years removed, that such irritability in me is the exact opposite of a sign of maturity.)

I waited out my two years more of Sunday school. My first year of confirmation class was, shall we say, difficult for everyone involved. I was frustrated I'd had to wait so long, and angry that my peers were not as passionate as I was about declaring our spiritual independence. I was thrilled by study of the Scriptures and the catechism; they were less so. I knew I'd lost the battle the day our youth minister said, in the self-deprecating tone adults sometimes take when trying to appeal to teens: "Sure, I read the Bible cover to cover when I was your age, but I was a giant nerd." I had hoped that at least within the bubble of Christian formation, my hunger for a deep dive into Scripture would have been satisfied. Instead, devotion like mine was something to chuckle at, to categorize as nerdy and toss aside.

I caused enough trouble in confirmation class that, in the second year, it was kindly suggested by Father Joe that I take on an independent study with him. This was a stroke of brilliance on his part, as I thought it was an honor and everyone else thought it was a relief. He tasked me, among other things, with writing additional questions for each section of the Episcopal catechism; we discussed my tentative thoughts about a possible call to ministry. I anxiously told him that my best friend had invited me to start attending her boyfriend's Bible study, and that they were *Lutherans*. I remember him sitting on my parents' couch, my cat contentedly rubbing against his legs, as he explained the diversity of denominations in Christianity: "We may all look different, as each cat looks different from another, but underneath the fur, the muscles and organs and bones, the core of who we are as Christians is all the same."

We were the last group Father Joe would confirm. In our confirmation class picture, on the day of Pentecost, his face is worn and grizzled with grey stubble. He was fighting throat cancer, and he passed away before we reached the next Advent.

I felt myself becoming untethered from my childhood church. I'd waited for so long to be an adult in my faith, but now that I'd claimed the responsibility, I was no longer sure. I watched as my confirmation class affirmed their faith before the whole congregation and then stopped coming to church at all. I saw the congregation as a whole struggle with the loss of our head priest and the turmoil of transition. My so-very-dangerous Lutheran Bible study taught me to pray out loud, unscripted, without the guide of a Book of Common Prayer. I added additional books to my study, like Misty Bernall's *She Said Yes: The Unlikely Martyrdom of Cassie Bernall*. I used my Columbia Records discount mailings to get *Now That's What I Call Worship! 2000*. I attended my first Teens Encounter Christ (TEC), the Episcopal version of Cursillo: a long weekend of spiritual immersion in testimony, song, Bible study, and fellowship. I was so enraptured by the passion, energy, and creativity embodied in TEC that I openly wept nearly the whole weekend. But when I went back to regular Sunday church, nothing had changed. The organ still rolled on. Father Joe was still gone. And the commitment I'd seen in other Episcopal teens from around the city was dispersed, each to their own congregation and me back to mine—where all my peers had already stopped coming.

"It's kind of far away," Rebecca said. "If you meet us at the donut shop you can ride with us."

"I'll ask my mom," I said, "but I think she'll say yes."

Mom did not, in fact, want to say yes, but I think she may have known better than to say no. Every teen has their rebellious phase; mine was to start attending an Assembly of God youth worship.

Rebecca got me to go simply because she asked. There was no particular selling point, no conviction about my need for salvation, no poking fun at my stoic mainline upbringing. She just said, "You want to come?" and I was floored that there might be a place with *other people my age who wanted to be there*. Rebecca also had glamour-long blonde hair and a charismatic personality, and no small part of me hoped that maybe church would redistribute some of the sparkle.

Watermark[2] was a place unlike any church I'd ever been in. A converted warehouse out in the exurbs of Saint Paul, the church was flat and square, with a lit-up steeple plunked on top. Inside was grey office carpeting and a coffee station, with childcare down one side hallway and the massive sanctuary directly ahead. It was a sprawling space, with dark draperies covering the cement stone walls and stage lights beaming up with red and blue. The altar was less altar and more stage, with a drum set behind a sound wall and a wide blank space for the projector. We sang songs I'd only ever heard through my headphones: "Here I Am to Worship," "Trading My Sorrows," "I Could Sing of Your Love Forever." I was surrounded by a hundred other teenagers tall on their feet, hands in the air in praise, eyes rapt on the lyrics or fluttering closed with silent tears as they mouthed the words they'd already memorized. Kids my age were playing in the band, with dirty sneakers pounding out the tempo. The preacher wore loose-fitting jeans and a dark grey T-shirt with a faded image of the church's logo. A dozen other adults floated around the space, laying a hand on the shoulder of one crying teen or standing with a small group to pray at the back.

I was both scandalized and enthralled. Ripped jeans on the altar! No bulletin or hymnbook to guide me! Just slide after slide flickering past, run by some unseen messenger of God in the back sound booth. Half the time the pulpit was just a music stand pulled from the guitarist, the youth pastor setting down his open Bible with sticky notes cluttering the page and pacing the stage as he spoke, one hand white knuckled on the handheld mic. And all around me a hundred or more other teenagers, eager and passionate. They took their shoes off to "stand on holy ground" as worship began. They were anxious to run forward and play a toned-down version of Fear Factor between the music and the sermon. They took furious notes in the wide margins of their study Bibles. They clutched each other's hands as they prayed fervent whispers, their worries and hopes spilling out to Father God.

All of the passion and energy and emotion I'd experienced at Teens Encounter Christ; all the zeal for the Bible I'd read about in the martyrdom accounts of Cassie Bernall; all the music I'd been memorizing on drives to school before I picked up friends and switched out my Jennifer Knapp CD for my equally worn CD of *Rent*; everything I had been hungering for in confirmation, in the years of waiting to be accountable for my own faith, held to a standard, expected to participate: here it was.

I attended Watermark for the better part of two years. I learned what it was like to live in two worlds. I was fighting my way through depression with therapy and medication. In school, I was still struggling to feel accepted, moving between multiple friend groups. I agonized over whether my choir solo or my competitive speech piece would ever make me likeable. But at Watermark I didn't feel I had to pretend. I didn't feel strange or isolated when I cried; everyone there cried at some point. It didn't matter who my friends were, because we were *all* friends in Jesus. And of course I was accepted; everyone was.

But the biggest split in identity was that I was starting to come out. My parents showed no surprise when I first told them, the summer I was sixteen. The first words out of their mouths were "we love you no matter what." But they, like I, had taken the temperature of the culture and suggested I not tell my friends at school yet. I'd had a hard-enough time fitting in as a kid; I was doing okay, now, in choir and theater, but there were still no other openly gay kids and there was still a significant amount of prejudice.

I, unsurprisingly, thought I knew better. At first I was tentative, keeping a strict list of "who knew" in the front of my journal, making sure to control the spread of information. Eventually I learned this is not how high school works. I was outed, on a few occasions. Another girl pursued me and outed me to friends when I rejected her advances. I "fell in love" with a straight girl, which was disastrous all around. I went on my first—and only—high-school date with a girl. I wrote a lot of very bad poetry.

As I came out more and more, a few friends raised eyebrows, and one memorably told me, "But that's not okay. It's a sin. That's in the Bible." I blinked at her. What church was *she* going to? Sure, some people believed that, but they lived in far-off places like Georgia or Colorado or Utah. No one in suburban Saint Paul was that backward.

Slowly I was beginning to own my own story, to claim the word *gay* without feeling like I might throw up. Slowly . . . except at Watermark. My mother cautioned me one night as I headed out for the donut shop: "Honey, if you tell them who you are, they won't accept you."

I rolled my eyes. "Mom, they accept *everyone.*"

And yet the words never crossed my lips. I saw no reason to mention it. My sexuality didn't bother me; I didn't need to pray about it or ask for "guidance." I was learning about the courtship model, the newest branding of Christian requirements for abstinence until marriage. Courtship, as best known from the Joshua Harris series of books, required not only sexual and physical abstinence but emotional. We were not to date, to grow emotionally close with someone of the opposite sex, until God had made it clear that we were each other's destined marriage partner. For a gay girl who knew no other gay girls, this was pretty easy to sign on to. I wrote my own covenant, promising not to date until God told me I'd met the woman I was going to marry. Sure, this wasn't exactly what Harris had meant (several editions of the book, in fact, made very clear his opinions on "homosexual desire"), but I was a graduate of the elementary school Gifted and Talented program—I was accustomed to being smarter than the book. I told myself my covenant was a feasible work-around, the best option for being a gay Christian, really, if anyone asked—and I made sure not to let anyone ask. I think I knew my mother might have a point, but I certainly wasn't going to admit it.

In October of my senior year, almost two years since I'd started attending Watermark, the youth pastor announced that tonight we would be hearing from a preacher-in-training from the nearby Christian seminary. I felt my heart beat faster. I hadn't talked to anyone about my call to ministry since Father Joe had died. Seminary seemed like a dream I'd woken from, only half-remembered. The excitement I'd hidden for years began to resurface.

The seminarian, Todd,[3] took our youth minister's place at the podium. He had more notes than our youth pastor usually did—a whole handful of typed pages. When he walked back and forth, his feet fell so hard that they echoed in the empty space beneath the stage. He didn't open with a story; he launched right into the anger.

This world is a threat to you. This world wants to destroy you. Do you know about the threat? Have you clothed yourselves in the armor of God against the world that wants to eat you alive?

I was surprised by his vehemence. My notes in my sermon journal began to trail off.

There are so many evils assailing you. So many ways the Devil is trying to pull you away from Jesus. The first evil is alcohol . . .

I fully agreed with this. I'd seen enough late '90s after-school specials to know that kids my age were just laden with opportunities to get wasted and make bad choices. I'd done a group project on teen alcoholism in YA literature just the year before. One of the fictional kids' friends had *died*. (This is, truly, the closest experience I had to underage drinking in high school. It's not that my friends weren't having parties. They just didn't invite me, because they sensed I'd be a goody-two-shoes about it and probably tell their parents. I suspect they were not wrong.)

The second evil assailing America's youth today is abortion . . .

Here my notes paused again. As someone who had no opportunity to be sexually active, much less have to worry about pregnancy as a result, I'd never thought much about abortion. It wasn't talked about in my childhood church; it definitely wasn't discussed in my abstinence-only public-school health class. My only exposure was in the numerous *Your Changing Body!* books my mother had bought to supplement my education, where abortion had been described without being judged. I understood what he was getting at, but I had no experience to apply this to. Since I wasn't having sex, I had sort of assumed my friends weren't either. If anyone had had a pregnancy scare, I'd never heard about it. I wasn't sure who Todd was talking to.

But the greatest threat to our teenagers today . . .

I picked up my pen again. I'd been thinking a lot about this lately. There's something in the high-school structure, the cliques, the in-group–out-group nature of things that has to be sinful, doesn't it? It drives us from God to think we have to compete with each other. It makes us feel unwanted and worthless. I didn't know the right word for it: loneliness? isolation? exclusivity? I didn't know how to name it. I hoped, in that moment, that Todd would.

He pounded the plexiglass podium and shouted:
The single most sinful threat to your very lives . . .

is homosexuality.

––––––––––

The first thing I was aware of was my throat closing. I couldn't get a good breath. Rebecca, sitting beside me, turned slightly, looking at me. She knew—she'd heard through the rumors I couldn't control—but we'd never talked about it. I couldn't hear anything else Todd was saying; everything was simultaneously slowing down and speeding up. I closed my eyes. *God? Help. Help me. Please. Help me.* Nothing happened. No commanding voice, no revelatory light, not even a chasm to hell opening up beneath my feet to deliver me to eternal torment and spare me from this moment of knowing the truth about this place I'd come to love.

I didn't realize I'd stood up until I was in the aisle, slowly walking out. I made my way to the back door and slipped out, catching the door behind me so that it didn't thud as it closed. My bare feet met the strange hardness of the foyer carpet. I wasn't conscious enough to wish I'd grabbed my shoes; I was only aware of the sudden surge of tears down my cheeks, of enough air finally in my lungs to begin to sob.

I ran for the bathroom, locking myself in the last stall, pressing my hands into my face as I tried to stifle my cries, and also trying not to be grossed out by being barefoot in a bathroom. The words that came so easily to my lips during prayer time were gone. *God? God? Help me. Help me. Please.*

"Emmy?"

My heart flipped over. Someone else had come in. I succumbed to the momentary hope that it was the archangel Gabriel, but the voice was Rebecca's. I unlocked the stall door and came out, hoping she'd brought my shoes.

But it wasn't just Rebecca; Jess, one of the adult leaders, was with her.

"Emmy," Jess said, shaking her head, and the bottom dropped out of my stomach.

Rebecca wouldn't look me in the eye.

"Emmy," said Jess, again, gently, but firmly, like a mother holding back her wrath. I wanted my name out of her mouth. I wanted her out of this stupid bathroom. "Emmy, what sin has Satan laid on your heart that made you abandon worship?"

I couldn't answer.

"Well, I can guess at it, from when you left. What kind of wicked temptation is this?"

I couldn't answer.

She softened a little. "I was tempted too, you know, when I was your age." And so began a story I only half-heard, about figuring out she could gain the attention of boys by making out with a girl in front of them. There was something about divorce, something about wickedness, about sowing seeds when we are young that we can't uproot when we are old. Her words pounded against me, both unintelligible and deafening, relentless in their false kindness. This wasn't a gentle revealing of shared experience; this was a crafted explanation, with a direct path to the moral of the story.

"You know what you need to do, don't you?"

I couldn't answer.

"You need to pray the sinner's prayer. You need to turn to Christ and accept salvation. You need to turn away from this lifestyle of sin."

She let my silence hang in the air.

"So what do you want to *do*, Emmy?"

I did not yet know what *infallible* meant in a statement of belief.

I did not know how to explain that the books that comprise the Bible were written in separate times and places, by authors distanced by hundreds of years and a variety of religious and political circumstances. I had been taught that the Bible was a product of many authors, but I did not yet understand how multiple voices trying to confess to the same God did not magically align on all points across time and space.

I did not yet know that the six-day creation we were required to believe in was actually seven days. There are two creation accounts that go in a nearly opposite order—one where humanity, male and female simultaneous in the image of God, is made on the sixth day; one where Ha'adam, a genderless creature made of dirt, finds no partner in any of the created animals until God causes the earth-creature to sleep, takes its rib, and creates two humans, male and female.[4] I did not yet know Austen, now my best friend, who would teach me that "male and female," like day and night, sky and sea, water and land, did not preclude the existence of sunrise and sunset, rain and snow, beach and riverbank, and trans and nonbinary.

I did not yet know that the story of Sodom and Gomorrah is not a story of consensual gay relationships but violent gang rape against outsiders.[5] I knew only the barest of details, the most condemning ones: the men of Sodom wanted to have sex with the angels, and so the town was destroyed with fire and brimstone, just as all homosexuals would someday be destroyed. I had not yet started to lift up each detail of the story and wonder at it. The angelic messengers who have come to examine the city's supposed wickedness would have slept, homeless and unfed, on the ground in the center of town if Lot did not insist on extending his hospitality. The men of Sodom gathered, every single one of them, to demand that Lot turn over these visitors "that we may know them." The story does not reveal if these wicked men of Sodom demanded the bodies of the angels because they were so consumed with lust that they must overpower and penetrate every male-like body they saw, or because they thought the angels were aliens like Lot who needed to be taught their place. The men's motive is unimportant; the desire is clear: they would take these visitors by force, with no care for their host's cries nor for the visitors' own desires. I did not yet know this, that the parallels between Sodom and modern-day sexuality were far more about rape and power than about the gender of a partner (what gender *are* angels, anyway?).

I did not know how the prophet Ezekiel summarizes Sodom's sins: "she and her daughters had pride, excess of food, and prosperous ease, but they did not aid the poor and needy. They were haughty, and did abominable things before me."[6] I did not know that while there are the six or seven "clobber verses" interpreted to condemn homosexuality, there are hundreds of verses in the law of Moses and the cries of the prophets against injustice toward the orphan, the widow, the poor, and the stranger. I did not know how much my LGBTQ+ family knew what it was like to be orphaned, to be thrown out of the house by living parents livid at their no-longer-my-child's acceptance of their own truth. I did not know how many people, of all genders, I would come to meet who knew what it was like to be a widow: alone in a world designed for couples and families, singlehandedly providing for the vast needs of their children, struggling endlessly to catch up to those around them who had little compassion for how society had incapacitated those without a partner and a fellow provider. I did not know the myriad systems of economics and employment in America and around the world that repeatedly benefit those already well-off and isolate further those already at the bottom. I had not met many strangers, resident aliens in the land, those with immigrant histories far more recent than mine, whose wounds of civil war and political oppression were still fresh.

I did not know that Jude's condemnation of how Sodom and Gomorrah "indulged in sexual immorality and went after other flesh" is not a description of sins confined to same-gender relationships.[7] I had not yet heard the phrase, muttered by religion professors to come, of the Bible's lasting concern with "heterosexuals behaving badly." I did not know of the mirror story in the book of Judges, when an unnamed Levite is a guest in the town of Gibeah. When his host will not turn him over to the men of the town, they are given his concubine instead, whom they rape throughout the night. She dies on the doorstep. Her owner cuts her into twelve pieces and sends her to each tribe of Israel, demanding retaliation against Gibeah.[8]

I did not yet know that Leviticus is largely ignored by the Christian church except when it is convenient.[9] Nor did I know that Christians have imposed "cultural" and "ritual" distinctions on its laws that, conveniently, release the powerful from having to do anything uncomfortable but require the minority to practice lifelong celibacy.

I did not know that this church I had claimed for nearly two years had a long history of unresolved debate over women's preaching. I did not yet know how to point out the contradiction in a pages-long defense of the ordination of women but a refusal to apply the same scholarly debate to verses on homosexuality. I did not know how to question a church that practiced a "literal reading" of the Bible but happily joined their youth for after-worship fast food in a place that mixed beef with cheese and paid their workers far below a living wage. I did not know that there were far more verses about how to treat the poor, the oppressed, and the laborer than there were about homosexuality.

I did not yet know that five hundred years prior, the majority belief of the Western world and the Christian church was that the sun revolved around the earth. As telescopes and observational techniques improved, astronomers began to suggest that the sun was actually the center of the solar system and the earth moved around it. At first, the church rejected this outright. As the scientific community continued to study the stars and the sky, it became scientifically impossible to believe that the earth was the center of the universe. The church, then, had to recognize that the Bible verses that referred to the earth as "fixed," or observed the sun moving around the earth, did not reflect reality.[10]

I did not yet know that the Christian church in America, during the eighteenth and nineteenth centuries, was divided in its response to chattel slavery. Both pro-slavery and anti-slavery advocates had relied on verses and stories from the Bible to ground their political convictions. The Baptist church in particular split over the issue, and the anti-abolitionists formed the Southern Baptist Convention. Had not Paul himself said that slaves should submit to their masters "with fear and trembling," "wholeheartedly, fearing the Lord," regarding their masters as "worthy of all honor"? Were they not to show "complete and perfect fidelity" and always defer to their masters, "even to those who are harsh"?[11]

I did not know anything about the complexities of rendering ancient Hebrew and Greek into modern-day American English. I did not know how to say that God had not personally reached down from heaven to hand out copies of the New International Version. I did not yet know that *homosexuality* as a word and an orientation was not defined until the eighteenth century. I did not know the complexities of translating *malakoi* and *arsenokoitai*. I did not yet know that Paul's condemnation of same-gender sexual activity was influenced not only by the laws of Leviticus but also by the practices of the Greco-Roman culture around him.[12] Homosexuality was not an orientation; it was, at best, a behavior. Sometimes it was taking young boys as mentees under trained scholars who would dominate them both academically and sexually. Sometimes it was post-battle rape by the invading army, declaring victory over their defeated rivals with rape and murder. It was not an orientation; it was not a long-term consensual relationship; it was not a marriage; it was none of the things I dreamed of when I tried to imagine my future with another woman.

I did not yet know that Romans 1:26 is one verse in a larger rhetorical argument. Paul sets up sinners of the greatest abominations, who begin with worshipping creation rather than the Creator even though they knew God. Because they practiced ritual idolatry, God gave them up into "degrading passions" contrary to nature and then into every kind of wickedness: envy, lies, haughtiness, murder; they are "foolish, faithless, heartless, ruthless." Paul depicted these idolaters as the worst of all sinners and then attacked his hearers for judging them: "Therefore you have no excuse, whoever you are, when you judge others!" It was a setup for Paul's argument throughout Romans: salvation is based entirely on Christ, not on our own ability to do good works.

I did not yet know to question whether Paul's depiction of "unnatural" sexual desire still applied if we took scientific and psychological progress into account. If I *was* gay—if I was somehow innately attracted to women, if sexual orientation could not be converted through prayer and therapy—wouldn't it be unnatural for me to have sex with men?

I did not yet know the summary I would come to hear in my Lutheran college courses: "We take the Bible too seriously to take it literally." I did not know how college Christianity would enfold me, making space for both my passion for Scripture and my desire for integrity and justice. I did not know how I would bring my full self to college, how eventually I would be openly queer and Christian and repeatedly affirmed in calls to leadership and ministry. I did not know how I would meet other women who liked women, that we would have dinner dates and go on long walks in the cross-country fields and kiss in public. I did not know the call to ministry would come back again and again, the hold on my heart unbreakable, until I gave up on the pretense of waiting for the magical "right" time and just enrolled in seminary and trusted the Spirit to get me through. I did not know that before seventeen more years of life had passed, I would be ordained to congregational ministry, with my mother and my future wife side-by-side to set the stole around my neck.

I did not yet know any of this. All I knew was that I was barefoot in a public bathroom, my seventeen-year-old face streaked with tears.

"So what do you want to *do*, Emmy?"

I took a single shuddering breath.

"I want to go home."

I walked from the bathroom. I heard Jess call my name, but I did not turn. Rebecca caught up to me, said she'd get my shoes and meet me in the car. I walked outside and leaned against the hood of her Crown Royal until worship was over and we could leave.

There was a lot I didn't know yet. But I knew then that I could never go back.

CHAPTER 4

After that day, it is unsurprising that I developed a spiritual allergy to the word *sin*. It made me itchy and tense. I would feel sick for days on end, my stomach in upheaval, my palms sweating. The church's unquestioned use of words like *pure* and *righteous* and *holy* began to sting, like repeated blows on a bruise that could not heal.

In the Lutheran tradition (which I now claim as my own), there is an inclusion from the Catholic Mass on Ash Wednesday: *Most holy and merciful God, we confess to you and to one another, and before the whole company of heaven, that we have sinned by our fault, by our own fault, by our own most grievous fault, in thought, word, and deed, by what we have done and by what we have left undone.*

A traditional definition of sin is an action that either hurts others or harms our relationship with God. Sin is the opposite of the love to which Jesus commands us, the love of God and love of neighbor. This way of understanding sin sees it as synonymous with pride—being focused on our own wants more than the needs of others. Martin Luther called it *incurvatus in se*, the state of being turned inward toward the self and its desires, rather than outward toward our neighbor in need. The psalmist bowed his head: *Indeed, I was born steeped in wickedness, a sinner from my mother's womb.*[1] We are not oriented toward others or toward God as we are meant to be, this traditional definition says; we are oriented sinfully, wretchedly, abhorrently toward our own self.

This is not a sin I was taught to have.

I was raised in a progressive home. But I also grew up in a household with a sick father who struggled with his chronic pain by drinking. As much as my mother tried to shield me from his illness and encourage me toward independence, I sometimes had to play the third adult in the house. We worked around Dad's hospitalizations. I learned to curate my own feelings in order not to trouble him or Mom. The searing pain that clung to his nerves for years left him without many emotional reserves to raise a tender-hearted and increasingly depressed daughter. I had to learn to take care of him even as I needed to be taken care of.

Prideful self-orientation is not a sin I, assigned female at birth, was taught to have. This is not a sin that women are socialized to have access to. We are not trained to be self-oriented; we are encouraged to be helpers, associates, caregivers, self-sacrificing. We are trained, from the start, to be oriented toward others. To be told that we are prideful (because, we are told, all humans are sinfully prideful) is a message that does not match the roles most American women are culturally provided. This traditional definition of sin is more likely based on men's experiences and the experiences of those who have power and privilege—people who have the opportunity to self-define. Because we—women, but also people of color, queer people uninclined to call attention to themselves, and the many people disenfranchised by socio-economic pressures that tell them they can't achieve beyond a certain status—are so often coached into helper roles, we don't come to faith with a personal history of being turned toward ourselves and our wants; our worlds have often been defined, from the very start, by what we're expected to do for others, not ourselves.

I learned in seminary that one word used for this forced brokenness is *fragmentation*. Essentially, when we come to worship, study the Bible, or join in the practices of Christian community, we do not always come as whole people. Many of us are coming as people who have already received a message, in multiple insidious cultural forms, that we are in some way defective or sub-ideal.[2] Around the same time I learned these things about sin, I was also exposed to the social-studies work of Brené Brown and the distinction between *guilt* and *shame*. Guilt says "I did wrong"; shame says "I am wrong." This distinction echoed within me like a shockwave blast.

The church had turned a crucial part of my identity into sin. There was nothing I could do to rid myself of my sexuality—first, because I was not convinced it *was* sinful, but second, and much more consequentially, because *orientation and identity cannot be changed.* Psychological and psychiatric science had been confessing to this since the 1970s, when homosexuality was removed as a treatable diagnosis from the *Diagnostic and Statistical Manual of Mental Disorders.* I knew it less because science "confirmed" it and more because the word *gay* had resounded within every fiber of my being. At fourteen, when I'd first tried the word on, it wasn't a name for my actions or experiences, nor something that had been "done" to me by family or trauma that could, with enough therapy and time, be undone. It named the way I moved in the world, how I related to others and to myself. It was as much a part of me as my dark hair, my love for books, the way my heart is inexplicably fed by being close to running water dappled with sunshine. Guilt could be alleviated through repentance and amends, through looking at the actions I'd taken and the causes behind them and taking steps to repair the damage and prevent future harm. There was nothing for that in my sexuality.

When the church and its leaders stood against me and declared my innate being an affront to God, I had no recourse. There was nothing to "do" or "undo." There was only the long stretch of a lonely future ahead of me, never to be in a relationship, never to have children or grandchildren, to be constantly on guard against temptation, to sever a core part of myself and pray that, with enough time, it might wither and die. The difference I had already begun to feel, the separation from others, was now turned into a promise of eternal isolation. There was no chance of redemption. I was so broken internally that no amends could be made.

Our culture has progressed significantly from twenty years ago when I was a baby gay; I didn't know there would come a day when there would be *multiple* role models on a national scale for what it meant to be a gay woman, much less my sisters who are queer and trans, my gay and bisexual and trans brothers, my nonbinary siblings, the people of color among our queer family. The progress made has not changed the fact that the process of self-discovery and then self-revelation ("coming out") is still intense, painful, terrifying, and even dangerous for many queer and trans people. When I as a gay Christian was subject to liturgy or music or Scripture or preaching that declared "you are a sinner who can only be saved by grace," it was meant to be a radical reversal of prideful self-centeredness. But I was coming to faith already fractured, and this declaration was not some awakening to the pride that had turned me away from others or from God; it was rather a confirmation of just how wretched I already knew I was. The proclamation of my sinful nature was meant to be a gift that freed me from my self-orientation, but my self had already been taken from me; the gift of "sin" weighed down like an unbearable yoke.

I am now thirty-three years old. I was first diagnosed with "stress-induced depression" when I was fourteen, and I can trace depressive episodes back to at least the age of ten. My mental illness is now old enough to drink (which is, for the record, a substandard way of celebrating depression).

There were years when I was so wrought with social anxiety that I could not walk into a grocery store. The idea of that many strangers in one place, that many interactions, that many possible judgments on which brand of spice I had chosen—no. I couldn't go in. I would sit in my car, staring at the automatic doors, shivering in the growing cold until I gave up and texted my girlfriend to ask her to get milk for me when she got off work. I don't think she ever understood (although she was always kind about it); I knew my terror was irrational. I knew, logically, that I was not interesting enough for strangers to judge me; even if they did, they likely wouldn't say it out loud; if they *did* say something, it was on them, not me; and even if someone started raging at me in the self-checkout for taking too long to scan a label, I was not going to die.

I knew all this. I was convinced I was going to die anyway.

Depression and anxiety are not uncommon codiagnoses; one can contribute to another, or they can happen at the same time. (This is called comorbidity, which is not the best medical phrase ever, in my opinion.) My depression has been a companion all my life; the anxiety was a new introduction, somewhere around age twenty-five, and medication finally got it on the run at age twenty-eight, although it still strikes on a lower level in high-stimulus situations with a lot of strangers (like a grocery store). Like all physical conditions, positivity can help but it cannot cure. Just as with the prayers we offer over every other physical disease, from cancer to Alzheimer's to substance abuse, positivity can make a difference, even extend recovery or prolong life, but it cannot cure—and I know this from twenty years of fervent prayer. Regular exercise and sunshine and green vegetables and time with friends have offered significant improvement in my life, but so does medication, and none of the above have made my depression disappear for good.

As a child, I was diagnosed for a few years with exercise-induced asthma. If I ran too hard or too long, my lungs would suddenly clench, and my throat would rasp and close. My hands froze up, half-clenched, struggling to move as my blood oxygen began to slowly drop. At first I would frantically gulp cold water, trying to relieve the crushing pressure in my chest, but the water dropped uselessly into my stomach and my airway still constricted. My throat would be momentarily soothed and then immediately seize taut again. It appears to have been a long-standing lung issue aggravated by construction in my elementary school; a few years later it faded, and I built up the endurance to run a seven-minute mile by high school. In between those years, I came to rely on my inhaler, pumping the medicinally laden bitter air into my contracting lungs. The relief was never instant, like the commercials had promised; it took a while for my body to recover from losing air.

My experience of depression has been similar. I am emotionally and mentally running hard, my thoughts pounding a metaphysical pavement, body and mind in tune with the project and its goal. Without warning everything stops. My body and mind seize. I slow to a walk, a crawl, sometimes only the couch. My hands struggle to move, undirected and unproductive. My mind, usually swimming with ideas, is suddenly drowning in a slow-motion video of every way I have failed, every reason I will never be lovable. I am mentally surrounded, for hour upon hour, by my inadequacies, my mistakes, my faults, my own faults, my own most grievous faults. But unlike the psalmist who could call on God and feel relief, I find no freedom in faith, only more grey fog, only more numbness.

Depression has a number of potential causes, as diverse as its sufferers. For some it attacks out of nowhere. Mine has almost always remained within the category of "stress-induced"; another therapist suggested it was best understood as a lack of emotional resilience. (I did not love this suggestion, but I cannot deny its reality.) Simply put, when disaster strikes—a bad week at work, a crisis in a relationship, the death of my father—I do not bounce back emotionally within what is considered a "normal" timeline. In middle and high school, the fog was so consuming that I could not function socially, to the point of calling from school once a week begging my father to come pick me up because I was "sick." I spent an entire summer on the couch watching the same three Bogart and Bacall movies every day, because I could not find the inner strength to move. I passed my honors calculus and chemistry classes on homework alone, nearly failing each exam because my mind blanked on simple math. In seminary, when I was living in my friend Natalie's basement, she'd leave her dog at home when she went to work, knowing that feeding and walking him might be the only way I could pull myself out of bed that day.

Religious responses to mental illness have often catego-
rized it as sinful: self-indulgent, self-oriented, a twisted sense
of pride to be so focused on my own wretchedness. Unlike
the word *gay*, this label unlocked no change in me. I didn't
want to be this self-oriented. I would love to be able to walk
the aisles of a store without my heart pounding and my body
temperature escalating until I am covered in sweat. I would
love to be able to get out of bed, to move, to eat in a way that
is nourishing to my body, to go to class with a clear mind, to
spend time with others without a clouded heart. As far as I can
tell, one of the attractions of sin is that it's relatively enjoyable.
Depression and anxiety are the opposite, like a beast that has
woven its claws into my skin and cannot be extracted. There is
no fun, no high, no enjoyment found in being so emotionally
raw that I will weep unstoppably at nearly anything. I am not
indulging; *I cannot do anything else.*

As early as the second century, the Christian church
soundly rejected as heresy the idea that the mind could be
divided from the body. Some taught that the body was to be
treated as suspect, even dangerous; the goal was to separate
the inward self from physicality, to imitate Paul in separating
flesh and spirit in order to better achieve union with the divine.
There were numerous reasons that the church rejected this
idea (later termed *Gnosticism*), not all of them religious. But
what particularly spoke to me was the church's assertion that
body and spirit could not be divided. Somehow, in dealing
with mental illness, the church has slipped back into believing
in a clean body/mind split. Constant assurances that I'd be

"cured" if I prayed harder or believed better or bought more hand-lettered frames with "Can any of you by worrying add a single hour to your life?" were well meant, but they denied a core understanding of the Christian faith: the flesh means something. The reality, much less convenient for me or for those trying to "help," was that I was a full person: heart, soul, mind, and body. God, in fact, had been one of those too. For the greatest act of mercy, for the pinnacle of the proclamation of the divine, God had put on flesh and walked the earth—had stubbed his toe, had hammered his thumb, had known hunger and thirst, had experienced sadness and anger and joy and pain. For the church now to act as if God's incarnation was a key part of the salvation story but deny my existence in a body that happened to significantly benefit from ten milligrams of citalopram seemed disingenuous at best.

The benefit, I noticed, was that when the church called my mental illness a sin, it became my burden alone to carry. There was no consideration of the roots of my depression, no accounting for how it might have found its place in me. The religious systems of power that encouraged women to churn out cross-stitched pillows with "Weeping may last for the night, but joy comes in the morning!" had no desire to hold themselves accountable to the ways they had played into my suffering. Medication helped, but so did therapy—especially therapy that simultaneously took my religious convictions and my sexuality seriously. When mental illness was a sin, a fault of my own, a failure of my faith, my neurologically compromised brain heard over and over again that my self was a sin, and

I was irredeemable unless I was perfectly abstinent from my own identity. Coupled with the assertion that sin and temptation would be ever-present and that only Jesus could save me from myself, I came to know that I was both required to be perfect and that I never would be.

———

The more my worldview has expanded, the more I have come to know the lie of isolation. I am not alone in feeling that my orientation made me unlovable and unacceptable, but even more so, I am not alone in feeling the weight of the church's dictates in a way that, instead of freeing me, broke me further. I have come to recognize many of the same scars of spiritual abuse and neglect not only in those who, like me, have had their sexuality or gender identity weaponized against them, but also in those who have experienced physical or sexual assault. The ravages of assault, especially sexual assault, on a survivor's psyche are soul-splitting enough without the judgment imposed by the church. The purity culture that dominated the evangelical church when I was a teenager and young adult was yet one more assertion by an institution run by men that women were the problem. We were the problem because we were too sexy and therefore attracted attention. We were the problem because we were not sexy enough and therefore doomed our husbands into temptation. We were the problem because we had sex before marriage. We were the problem because we didn't know how to please a man in bed. We were the problem because we let the abuse go on too long. We were the problem because we didn't forgive our abuser. There was no conversation around sexual ethics outside of heterosexual marriage, of course, which meant for those of us hiding our sexuality, the secrecy and shame was tripled, as is the concurrent rate of mental illness.

In witnessing the trauma wrought upon survivors of sexual assault, I could not stop thinking of Jesus. Jesus, sitting on the side of a mountaintop, saying not *if her lipstick causes you to sin* . . . or *if her yoga pants* . . . or *if her sexuality* . . . but *if your eye causes you to sin* . . . Jesus firmly rejects the objectification of women, puts the lustful eye of men on the level of adultery, and then *makes it the man's obligation.* Jesus, the man at the center of my faith, God-in-skin, rejects the misogyny that runs rampant through our judgment of sin. He knew better, I think. He knew that judgment is rarely objective. When the religious elite came dragging a woman "caught in the very act of adultery," I wonder if he wondered: *and the man? Where is he? Truly I tell you, it takes two to tango.*[3]

Sexual, physical, and emotional abuse has long been shrugged off by the church as a problem for the survivor to carry. Not only has abuse been reframed as the fault of the victim, it has been perpetuated in the cloak of redemptive suffering: *well, we all have our cross to bear.*[4] Citing Jesus's call to discipleship, ministers (often cis men) have refused victims and survivors (often women) the right to accuse their attackers or divorce their husbands. Mental illness has been framed this way, too, suggesting that the struggle is beautiful because it unites us with Jesus. I value the solidarity of my Savior in my hours of darkness, but there is nothing inherently redemptive in suffering, especially if that suffering could be avoided with treatment and with justice. My best understanding of core Christian tradition around the cross is that Jesus did it *for us*. He died for us, because of us, instead of us. There is benefit and freedom in the cross. What is the benefit and freedom in my depression? No one is saved through it. No one is transformed, redeemed, given new life by my inability to sleep or to wake or to work.

No one is saved, too, by a survivor's acquiescence to further violence. There is a Christian narrative, especially in the modern era, that lifts up nonviolent resistance and passive submission to violence as the way to peace. My fellow white Americans, in particular, love a passive image of Martin Luther King. But nonviolent resistance is effective when it shames the violator—when witnesses see it and cry out and begin the work of justice. There is no salvation and transformation in silent, unseen suffering, borne day by day and year by year and generation by generation by those who are powerless. I will confess to the existence of miracle stories in which a husband, long-violent, is suddenly transformed by his wife's patient suffering; I will also witness to my years in Al-Anon (a program for the families and friends of alcoholics) that this story is not the norm and never a guarantee. The statistics show a woman who submits herself to beating again and again without recourse or protection is not likely to transform her abuser; she is likely to die at his hands.

The more I came to know the stories of my Christian family on the edges, the more I refused to believe that my mental illness, my isolation, anything in my body or in the world that broke me or others was a cross to bear. No one was benefiting from that cross. But I could see who benefited from making it mine to bear. It was easier, far easier, for the church to push off the burden of recovery and reconciliation on the survivor rather than to account for how we have created the system in which the violence could take place. When sin was a singular act between two people, it was easy to check off the resulting boxes. Had the sinner repented? Had the victim forgiven? Done and done, let's move on. When sin was a single person's balance sheet, the solution was simple. When sin was understood as the result of multiple factors, none of which a sole person could be assigned full culpability for, the solution became hazy.

There are few praise and worship songs confessing how we participate in the brokenness of others through systems of oppression. There is rarely a single word in prepared liturgies to remind me that just because I didn't cause the particular action that hurt a particular person, I am not freed from the communal problem. When I raise my voice on Good Friday to shout the words of the Jewish crowd *His blood be on us and on our children!*, the church has left it up to me to know that those words were used as the seeds of Christian bigotry, hatred, and pogroms. When Jesus turned to the religious elite and said *Woe to you, scribes and Pharisees, hypocrites, whitewashed tombs!* there was no asterisk with "not all Pharisees" noted in the margin.[5] If the system was complicit in the oppression of widows and orphans, if the religious authorities continued to exalt themselves and burden others, its participants were not spared from judgment.

Mary, too, knew this. The Spirit opened her mouth to sing of God's coming reign of justice: *God will send the rich away empty.*[6] Not just the evil rich, not just the selfish rich, but all who have benefited from a system in which some are on top and many more are on the bottom. Sin is communal, not only when we participate in or benefit from systems of oppression but also when we are content or lazy enough to stand by. The prophets cry out against this. My queer experience cries out against this. I do not have the benefit of saying "not my circus, not my monkeys" because I have known what it is like to experience oppression through others' sinful actions and to have friends, colleagues, those whom I have trusted stand aside and say nothing.

I know what it is to be a liability. Association with me and mine is far too suspect. I have come to expect rejection from churches that draw a clear dividing line; I know how to do a keyword search for *inerrant* on a church website before daring to cross a new threshold. But it is the ones who have called me friend, who have sent congratulations on my engagement, who call me sister and themselves ally and yet fall silent when the time comes to speak, who wound me the most. Some speakers and organizations who stand for Christian "progressivism" on such controversial topics as war and poverty make no space in their platform for LGBTQ affirmation, unless it is paired with a counterargument for "traditional biblical marriage." (This is, to my false shock, never an argument for polygamy, slave concubines, levirate marriage, or strict celibacy except in rare cases of "burning.")[7] Other "allies" simply do not know the theological hurdles I have to predict in every new location. I have had to ask friends if they know the conference they've invited me to is hosted by a church that openly declares my abhorrence before God. "I didn't even think about that," they'd respond. "I know," I'd want to answer. People who still claim my friendship continue to give time, money, energy, and social-media appreciation to churches that deny my humanity.

Every time I have heard the church's call for my lifelong celibacy, I remember Naomi returning to Bethlehem. Naomi and Ruth have sometimes been lifted up as an example of female love in the Scriptures; the promises Ruth makes, her hands tight on Naomi's sleeve, have been part of wedding ceremonies for thousands of years. (Ruth's covenant with another woman is still quoted in Scripture readings in marriages done by churches that abhor and condemn female-female relationships. The world is strange.) As stunningly powerful as Ruth's promises are, I was equally drawn to Naomi's vow only a few verses later. Her husband and sons gone, Naomi faces a future full of sorrow. Even the presence of her daughter-in-law does little to allay her suffering. Naomi is without her family, and her devoted daughter-in-law is a Moabite who will likely be ostracized in their Hebrew community. She has nothing to look forward to. *Do not call me Sweet*, Naomi says to the women. *Call me Bitter, for the Almighty has dealt bitterly with me.* I knew what it meant to be bitter, to have a "whole town stirred," to shake my head and push my friends away. *Is that you?* they ask. *No,* I want to respond. *Whoever you thought you knew is buried under devastation. She left her wholeness back somewhere else. Stay away from me, for I am no longer who I once was.*[8]

The brutality of others' silence and apathy is a test to my faith far more than my mental illness has ever been. I know Job's cry against the friends who condemned him: "What is my strength, that I should wait? What is my end, that I should be patient?" Although I am loath to impose a mental-health diagnosis on those who have not been seen by a doctor, Job certainly experienced the anger, despair, and doubt that I have come to know so well. Job faced the unremitting grief of losing pretty much everything in his test of faith. At my bitterest, I envied him. At least Job had the chance to have a family. His wife even survived Job's deliverance into the hand of the accuser. I did not know that I would even have that chance.[9]

To call my depression a "test of faith" is to belittle the concept. Job, at least, got an answer. We don't know how long he waited; twenty years in, I am still waiting. When the church tells me that my mental illness is a test of my faith, when pastors join their voices with Eliphaz and Bildad and Zophar to proclaim my suffering, my total brokenness, is something I wrought on myself, I wonder: *where is my whirlwind?* Where is my God who rends the heavens to tell me the pain is over, the fortunes restored?

Of course, a God who rends the heavens is not the God I have come to know. I have not yet seen mountains tremble. If

I have heard the voice of God, it has been only in the midst of sheer silence, a whisper without wind. God has not been a God of dominance, of earth-shaking ear-splitting declarations. For a long time this left me discomforted and unresolved; if God had spoken so clearly in ages past, why the silence now? But as I have developed a more intimate relationship with the Scriptures, I have seen my truth reflected back. God spoke, yes: to Moses from the burning bush, from the cloud on Mount Sinai, through the voices of the prophets and the person of Jesus.[10] But just as much—or even more—God has been silent.

The Israelites saw the divine in a pillar of cloud by day and a pillar of fire by night, but it was the voice of Moses that bore God's message.[11] The prophets cried out, but it was in their own voices and their own tongue. The psalmists wept, begging God for response, for recompense, for protection against enemies; they grabbed God by the collar and said, "You promised." There was no response from heaven, but there was conviction within themselves: *Be strong, and let your heart take courage, all you who wait for the Lord.*[12] The psalmist found her own voice to answer her prayer: *Save me according to your steadfast love.* I wrapped myself in the words of Psalm 88, the only lament psalm that ends without resolution: *You have made friend and neighbor shun me; all my companions are shrouded in shadow.* There was comfort in knowing that even my own devastation, the seeming end of my joy, did not go without a voice in Scripture.

Many of the stories that make it into the records of Scripture are full of drama and dialogue, with a bold flash of lightning and a thundering voice from heaven. They are crafted around the moments that change everything, the crash of transformation, the moment that divides forever *before* and *after*. Those of us who live with mental illness know what it is like to wait for those moments, to knit our white-knuckled fingers and beg for the word or sign or pill or therapy session or yoga pose that will split our soul irrevocably from the torment of depression or anxiety or trauma. We are waiting on our whirlwind. And the truth is, it rarely comes. The dust is shaken up around our feet not by a storm from heaven but by our own stumbling steps. We make our way toward healing moment by moment, each year finding a new point at which we can set up a memorial to say "I made it this far." There are glimpses of God, far less majestic than we may have wished and far more than many others get to see: a flash of light amid the fog, a whisper on the breath of the wind.

Once when I prayed, asking for direction, I imagined myself in a room, and the room began to expand far more than I could have anticipated. Each wall was white, and it was endless and yet still contained, and it seemed the whole world was waiting—not on a God to drop down from the sky with an answer neatly gift-wrapped, but only on the next inhale and exhale of my own small breath. We are not left alone, not even in the sheer silence of everything that seems impossible to face. We are breathed into by the one who made breath, and the world waits for us to move again.

CHAPTER 5

It all happened because of a bus.

I started college an Episcopal, after my disastrous experience elsewhere. There was a sweet little Episcopal church in our small college town of Northfield, Minnesota. It had white wood trim with black wrought iron on a bright red door. It wasn't home, but it was close enough, and although the thirty-minute walk would be rough in the winter, there was a shuttle that ran on Sundays from campus to a few blocks from the church. There was a chapel on campus, of course, with daily services and a Sunday worship with communion, but it was a *Lutheran* service, and I was *Episcopal*.

But that first Sunday, I missed the shuttle. I'm not sure to this day if I was late or the shuttle was early; either way, I missed it, and my roommate Liz suggested I skip the walk and just come to church on campus.

I hadn't told Liz, or anyone else, that I was gay. This was 2003. No state in the United States yet recognized same-gender marriage. Ellen DeGeneres had come out, her show had tanked, and the best role she'd landed since then was voice actor in a kid's movie about fish. And now I shared a bathroom with twenty-three other girls whose allegiances were unknown or, worse, openly shown to be antagonistic toward people "like me." The truth I'd slowly and then proudly borne in high school was quietly tucked away again, too risky to reveal. I did not have a plan for this. I only had a plan to not be that lonely fifth grader again.

I had a much more important plan than hiding my sexuality: to change the world for good through the proclamation of the good news . . . of middle-school choir. I'd been an above-average high-school alto with ten years of piano lessons. I also liked kids. This, I felt, was enough reason to choose a career in music education.

I did not, actually, want to be a music teacher. I did not necessarily *want* to be anything; what I'd experienced instead was a grasping. Every Sunday in church I felt something catching at my heart, as light as fishing line and as thick as a construction-crane lifting hook, pulling me compassionately but resolutely toward the pulpit and the altar. I wanted to preach, to preside, to help people. But I was skittish, now. I'd told Father Joe, but then I'd come unmoored from the church of my childhood.

The brief moment I'd thought about my call within the walls of Watermark had turned into a nightmare. That summer before college began, I watched a live feed of the consecration of Bishop Gene Robinson, the first openly gay and partnered man to be made bishop of the Episcopal Church. Gene's robe looked bulky, not quite right, certainly not befitting of the pomp of an Episcopal consecration—but necessarily so: he'd received enough credible death threats that under his clerics he wore a bulletproof vest. Middle-school choir seemed a safer way for me. It was not a choice I was conscious of; I had begun to grasp my call to ministry and then by degrees let it go again. If you had asked, I would have told you music was my primary passion and believed I was telling the truth.

But only weeks into the first of six semesters of music theory and I was drowning, spending hours on a single page of homework. The signs of my future failure were there. But I am nothing if not stubborn and had coupled that stubbornness with an impressive teenage ability to ignore my own inner compass's wild pull in a different direction. I'd chosen music education, dammit, and I wasn't going to fail.

Music was nearly impossible to escape at Saint Olaf, and it filled every corner of Sunday mornings. Worship in Boe Memorial Chapel was a soul-deepening experience of rich tradition, laden with artistry and care. The stained-glass windows along one wall captured the stories of the Old and New Testaments, with small marbleized accent glass on the swirling stars of creation or the shawl of a small child listening to the Beatitudes. Across the other wall, the mid-morning sun shone through the history of the church: the fire of Pentecost, the letters of Paul, and stories of men I had not yet come to know: Wycliffe, Huss,

Luther, Zwingli, Calvin. The wood pews were marked with age, their crafted curves now worn into softness by thousands of hands. The organ had two consoles, one at the front and one at the back, and two sets of pipes that, on their own, outnumbered most congregations' entire collection. At the organ most Sundays was John Ferguson—one of the best organists in the nation, I was often told—playing for a group of college kids in the middle of a cornfield in southeastern Minnesota.

It was the first time in my life I'd ever seen peers excited about an organ. Volunteers showed up two hours early to join the ad hoc choir on Sundays when one of the six campus choirs wasn't scheduled. The pews filled with teens and twentysomethings, fresh-faced, in dress pants or clean jeans, giddily waving to friends who'd come in late, scooting along the oak veneer to make more room. The hymnals were green and well worn in the middle; after forty years of use, the binding had been worn along the most frequently sung hymns, easily flopping open to "Beautiful Savior." I don't know if there is any other sound like four hundred college students who voluntarily gather at 10:30 a.m. on a Sunday to sing harmonies they've learned from birth. I do know that if heaven doesn't sound like it, I'm not going.

I gave up on the Episcopal church in town and kept going to Sunday chapel, although I protested any suggestion that I was "becoming a Lutheran." I'd learned from years of study that there were times to hide my difference and times to declare it with a smirk. Being the lone Episcopal in a sea of Lutherans was just enough difference to satisfy my need to be known without endangering me to any actual semblance of vulnerability.

This Sunday was Homecoming Week. We'd been crawling over alumni for two days now, making space for them in our late Friday classes that they wanted to visit, weaving around them in the cafeteria during Saturday lunch. Today they packed the chapel, and Liz and I squeezed into a side pew up front on the left. I stared up at the stained-glass child at the foot of the Sermon on the Mount, their shawl a whirl of blue and pink and clear frost. The artist hadn't shown if they were male or female, but their rapt attention to a preaching Jesus was certain.

Worship was nerve-tinglingly rich, as usual, compounded by the fullness of the chapel, which kicked the interior temperature and the musical volume up several more degrees. As we passed the peace with a significantly higher number of people than usual, Liz caught my elbow. "They need more help with communion. Come on."

I blinked, and then (as would often be the case in the coming three years of living with Liz and her joyous spontaneity) I followed. Through a side door we found the sacristy. There was barely anywhere to stand as a dozen other students darted around, handing off half-full pouring chalices and full pitchers and basket after basket of individual empty cups. Liz declared we were there to volunteer, and I stepped toward the back room where I saw a sink full of cups that needed washing.

Suddenly someone pushed a ceramic plate into my hands. It was heavy and cool, the polished rim pressing into my palms, the molasses bread upon it fresh from baking that morning. I looked down at the dark cross pressed into the loaf and immediately looked back up at the stranger who had handed me the plate. "I can't," I said, apologetic but clear.

In the church I'd grown up in, under the priest who had promised to help me explore my pull to ministry, there were clear guidelines about who was able to serve communion and who was not. To serve, one had to attend a weekend training and receive a certificate; to attend the training, you had to be confirmed (which meant you had to be sixteen or older) and you had to not be engaged in any high-school activities that required your presence elsewhere on a Saturday. In practice, only those over eighteen, and usually only adults well into their thirties and beyond, were communion servers, and only the priests or deacons distributed bread. This made perfect sense to me at the time. Communion was a remembrance of Christ's sacrifice for us, our participation in the foretaste of the feast to come; it should not be served without solemnity or taken without consideration. And I, at eighteen, had never been to training; I only could mouth along with the priest as she intoned: *Let the grace of this Holy Communion make us one body, one spirit in Christ, that we may worthily serve the world in his name.* "Risen Lord, be known to us in the breaking of the Bread," we would respond. Service was for all, but serving communion was for the chosen.

"I can't serve," I repeated. "I'm not trained." I tried to hand off the plate to the closest possible person—one of the campus pastors. This, I did not yet know, would be my downfall.

The senior campus pastor, Bruce Benson, had been there for thirty years. He stood over six feet tall and thin as a rail. He had a scraggly grey beard sprinkled with black; coupled with his deep and booming baritone, his likeness to an Old Testament prophet was a frequent comment among the chapel attendees. His eyes were blue and light, and they had two settings: the twinkle of compassion or the sparkle of snark. He had at least eight inches on me, and he looked down at me over his small oval glasses.

He took a moment, observing the situation as I held the plate out, my eyes declaring my unwillingness to be complicit in the unrighteousness being forced upon me. He half-took the plate back, and then peered at me again and asked: "Do you know what to say?"

I swallowed, and carefully answered, "T-the body of Christ, given for you."

He let go of the plate, and the full weight of it fell back into my hands. "There you go. You've been trained."

It could be argued that Pastor Benson simply needed to get one more set of hands ready. Perhaps his comment was not meant to be a theological assessment of the nature of the Eucharist. But in every moment since, in all that I have understood of Lutheran proclamation and practice, I have not yet found a sentence to better summarize what communion is.

Through the fifteenth century, Catholic teaching dominated western European thought in Christianity. In the consecration of the Eucharist, the elements were transformed into the body and blood of Christ, only appearing to still be bread and wine. At the last supper, Jesus had taken the simple bread of Passover and proclaimed, "Take, eat; this is my body." When Jesus declared he was the bread of life, he followed with the promise, "Very truly I tell you, unless you eat the flesh of the son of Man and drink his blood, you have no life in you."[1] Was it so impossible to say that Christ was showing up for us again, fifteen hundred years after the first promise?

The Reformers who preceded Luther, especially Wycliffe and Hus, challenged this traditional interpretation, preferring instead a symbolic interpretation of the Eucharist. Communion was a remembrance, a memorial, a reenactment of Jesus's final meal with his disciples, but not a promise of his presence in the elements. "Do this in remembrance of me," Christ had commanded.[2] If there was no visible change in the elements, how could it be said they had been substantially altered? If there was no promise in the Gospels of such a miraculous transformation, how could the church proclaim it, even insist on it? At best, if Christ *was* present, it would have to be called mystery; the church could make no authoritative declaration as to how Jesus was showing up in communion.

Luther stood in the gap, a devout Catholic monk of the Augustinian order, who read and understood the challenges of his contemporaries. He could not wholly reject the promise of Christ to be present in communion; he could not accept what seemed an extrascriptural interpretation that the elements were therefore fully and permanently transformed. Bread and wine were bread and wine. But in the act of communion, in the promise from priest to believer that "this is the body of

Christ, given for you," something grander than memory or symbol was taking place. Christ was fully present, impossibly so, in that moment of sacramental promise.

The transformation of the elements or the memory of the Last Supper became background for the work not of the priests or the believer but of Jesus: to be powerfully present in the moment of the Eucharist. An unworthy priest could still consecrate; an unworthy believer could still receive. It was not about the virtue, the knowledge, even the faith of the people involved; Luther saw humanity as far too fallible to bear that burden. It was Jesus, Jesus's promise, Jesus's power in which the beauty of communion rested.

From the day that plate first rested in my hands, the promise of sacramental union rang true for me. The training that the church of my childhood had required was worthwhile, no question; if we were truly handling the body and blood of Christ, it was better to do it with reverence. But it was not required. I was a baptized and beloved child of God; the rest was the work of Christ. The promise of Christ's real presence expanded the bread and wine beyond what I could hold. In the crumbs there was a proclamation of an impossibly expansive God.

The God present in the bread was the God who had freed the Israelites from slavery, who had broken the bonds of oppression and wealth and power to lead them across the sea on dry land. The God in my hands was the God who had sent quails to cover the camp at night and frost to cover it at dawn, the God who had left thin wafers of bread across the sand of the camp, the God who chuckled when the Israelites picked up the fine flaky substance and said to each other, "What is this? What is this?" This was the bread of impossibility, the bread of the promise that God could provide, that work and work and work and work was not the path to salvation or protection. *Manna*, the bread of the wilderness. This was the bread that made no sense and yet was there six days of each week for over two thousand weeks, skipping each Sabbath with a terrifying regularity, reminding the people again and again to rest. Each stale wafer that stuck to the roof of my mouth held the God who had fed the chosen people both with food and with freedom.

The God who found me in the communion chalice was the God who inaugurated his ministry with ridiculous abundance, with rich red wine at a wedding where everyone was already drunk. The God now held in my shaking, sweaty hands was the God who drank and ate with sinners. This was the God who had smiled with quiet pleasure at the religious expert who failed to understand the offensive nature of mercy, a God whose human feet had been washed by a woman with wet eyes and trembling hands. As Simon the Pharisee glared at the offense of a sinful woman at the feet of Jesus, this God had interrupted his internal rant. This God who I now held in my hands had proclaimed the nature of salvation: "She has anointed my feet with oil. Therefore her many sins have been forgiven; hence she has shown great love." What came first, I wondered, the forgiveness or the love? The mercy or the response to mercy? The bread or the body?[3]

Yes, communion answered me. There was no before and after. There was no twelve-step process to my betterment before the table of the Lord. There was no demand for perfect faith, for full comprehension, for my ultimate sanctification before I could be found worthy. Christ was there, waiting for me, the timeless Divine choosing to be bound in this moment. It was all there, element and substance together, the twinkling bright eyes of Pastor Benson as his fingers gripped the bread: *The body of Christ, given for you.*

On the first Easter, the day of impossibility, the first day the women and disciples could do anything besides sit and grieve, there was broken bread. The women had come and told their truth: an open tomb, a body missing, a flash of light, and two messengers with a proclamation: "He is not here, but has risen." The women had run to find the disciples, their words tumbling over each other, gasping with the exertion and elation and shock. But the men had shaken their heads, disillusioned or even disgusted with another set of women's foolish talk and idle tales. And so two had set off to Emmaus, a seven-mile journey, mournfully chewing over the morning's events, throwing questions and disappointments back and forth as they walked. "We had hoped he was the one to redeem Israel," they told a stranger who met them on the way, and the stranger laughed and called them mindless and slow-hearted. Moses and all the prophets had confessed to this coming prophet, his life and death and resurrection, and the stranger walked alongside them on the journey.

And in a flash, over a simple dinner, the truth was known: the women's witness was no old wives' tale. Christ was alive, risen from the dead, freed from the tomb; he was known to them in the breaking of the bread.

God was there, big enough to fit into a sip of wine, close enough to hold.

God was here. My job was to get out of the way.

I served the bread that day. My hands were so sweaty that I vacillated wildly between the fear I'd be struck dead by lightning for serving without proper training and the fear that I'd drop the plate. Neither happened, and I have barely let go of serving the bread since. I will freely confess that I may have been excessively captured by the revelation of the real presence of Christ.

I have been finding new and complicated layers to the communion experience since that day. Years later, when I was serving communion in a Lutheran church off-campus, a parent pulled me aside before church to explain that her children *would* be receiving communion today, thank you very much. I blinked at her. "I know the teaching of the church is that you have to *understand* before you can receive," she went on, "but do *any* of us really understand what's happening at communion?"

This mother's proclamation baffled me. None of this was about *understanding*, I thought. Who *could* understand what was happening here? Who has said we need to try? The promise isn't of understanding but of presence, not ours but God's. That was the entire launch-point of Luther—that it was the work of Jesus, and nothing of our own righteousness, that saved us.

The conclusion was singular and obvious. "Of course they'll receive," I answered.

When her four-year-old came forward with paint-stained stubby fingers outstretched, I instinctively knelt. I remembered how Pastor Benson had held the bread the first time I'd received from him: up and between us, so that I could see his face when he pronounced the words I knew so well. I also remembered an article I'd read three days before on child development and how important it was to be on a child's level when talking to them, rather than bending down over them. (At barely 5'5", the concept of being physically imposing is outside my experience, but I trust the theory.)

"Tommy," I said, balanced on one knee, holding the broken bread up between us so that he could see both it and my eyes in one glance. "This is Jesus, given for you."

He giddily reached out and took the body of Christ.

I began kneeling for every child. I broke bread and lifted it, pressed between my fingers, my eyes seeking others, trusting the theology of Lutheran practice: the presence of Jesus is in the moment of promise.

More years later, serving at my internship congregation, my supervising pastor Deb used everyone's name at communion; I began to as well, relying on nametags when my Sunday-morning brain failed me.

Gina, this is the body of Christ, given for you.

Jenni, this is the body of Christ, given for you.

Annie, this is the body of Christ, given for you.

When we gathered the children at the front for the kids' sermon every Sunday, there was bound to be some misbehavior. But the best was a three-year-old named Aiden, who craved communion so much he would sneak behind the altar table and steal bread. I am of the opinion that such faithful desperation is a perfect use of the Eucharist, but it was decided that for everyone's benefit, Aiden would be sitting in laps from now on—*and* we would be giving out any leftover communion bread when worship was done. Aiden would sit happily with a cookie in one hand and a hunk of bread in the other, chewing away while his brother headed off to Sunday school. I remembered my horror, years before, when I discovered that this was also how we disposed of the bread at Saint Olaf: we ate it. "It's Jesus in the moment it's given for you," said Liz, chomping away. "You don't have to be afraid of it after. You just have to respect it."

Matt, the body of Christ, given for you.
John, the body of Christ, given for you.
Deb, the body of Christ, given for you.

I looked into the thick molasses bread, the thin wafers, the rich red wine, and heard my name anew. I saw what it did, in the eyes of the people I served and loved, to be known by name. The gift of God came alive in that moment, the promised presence known. "For you" bore its true meaning and a new meaning all at once; suddenly it was real. In the breaking of the bread, God was known to us, and we were known to God. Christ was present with me, for me, in the palm of my hand. God was no longer far away, checking in to see if I was old enough, trained enough, righteous enough to give and receive the body of Christ. God was here, so magnificent and so abundant in joy to be found in something so simple as bread and wine. Christ had put on flesh, was born not only into a feed-trough in faraway Bethlehem but incarnate now, in the palm of my hand, reaching out for me as I reached out for him: *body of Christ, given for you.*

I first served communion with shaking hands and a stammering voice, an eighteen-year-old queer girl frantically closeted from both her sexuality and her pull to ministry. My fingers didn't know how to pull the bread apart. I forgot the words more than once, sucking in a trembling breath and closing my eyes to call them back. But every time I managed, fumbling and red-faced, to tear off another piece, I felt something in my heart grow larger and more irresistible. I came back the next week, and the next, stopping in the sacristy each Sunday morning: *can I help? can I help? can I help?*

As Christ became real for me, I became real for others. I came out to Liz, then to my friends. I started dating. I quit the music-education program and doubled up on religion classes. Three years later, I submitted my application for seminary. And each week, I reached for the altar and felt God reaching back for me. The hook in my heart no longer tugged but held me, making my feet more steady, my hands more ready, my mouth full of the words I'd been trained by a whole life to say: *body of Christ, given for you.*

What else could I have done? Jesus had shown up for me. It was no longer possible to hide myself away. Having held the bread once, I could never again pretend I was not called to it, that my heart was not both wrapped in dark golden bands of healing and cracked further open by every moment graciously given at the table.

Christ had promised to be present. All I had to do was get out of my own way, to stop believing that I or others were somehow unworthy to take and to share. If I confess with shaking and stammering faith that God, true God, light from light, has so desired to be close to me that I can reach out a hand and hold the majesty of heaven in my curved palm—if this is the confession of the Lutheran church to which I have been called and ordained for ministry, then I and we cannot stand in the way of others with the same trembling hands outstretched. My tradition confesses Christ crucified, Christ broken, Christ poured out for the whole world and found inexplicably in simple bread and wine. I do not know whether we should be more mystified by *how* the bread and wine can bear the presence of Christ or *how* we have come to know a God that loves and longs for us this much. But if this is Jesus, this simple bit of food and drink, then when we reach out for it, the eternal and immortal God is reaching back. God has never stopped reaching out for us. It is not our job to be worthy of it; it is our gift to receive, given with grace and abundance. The breath of the Spirit calls us by name, inviting us to the table where we receive a foretaste of the feast to come. The only task left for us to do is to get out of our own way.

CHAPTER 6

"You know, I was the *youngest* delegate to vote against gay ordination," he said proudly as his way of introduction.

It was my first day on campus at seminary, in September 2010. We first-year students had been sorted randomly into groups for dinner, shuttled off campus by faculty and staff who had volunteered to take us to one of Minneapolis's many good-but-inexpensive restaurants in order to foster greater fellowship. I'd climbed into someone's van only to be seated next to a guy, younger than me, who wanted to make sure everyone knew exactly how he felt about last year's decision.

In 2009, the Evangelical Lutheran Church of America's thirty-year debate over "homosexual ordination" came to a head at the national conference, where nearly a thousand pastors and lay delegates representing sixty-six congregational collectives had assembled. I watched the live stream as, after testimony after testimony, the vote was called: *Would the church eliminate the prohibition against ministry by members in publicly accountable, lifelong, monogamous same-gender relationships?* By a 68 percent majority, the motion passed.

Some voted against it because they felt it did not go far enough. A little-used concept called *bound conscience* had been introduced, allowing for congregations and members of the ELCA who felt that those in same-gender relationships could not be called to ministry to persist in their conviction. No church would be forced to consider same-gender-partnered candidates when looking for a new pastor—unlike, in the 1980s, when the ordination of women was a mandate across the ELCA, and congregations were required to at least see a slate of pastoral candidates that included women. Some who voted against the motion that day believed that the church should not attempt such a middle ground; it would only lead to continued internal division and likely to a surge of LGB-identified candidates in seminary who then found there were not enough churches that would accept their ministry. But most who voted against the motion were like the young man seated beside me in the van: vehemently opposed to the ordination of gay, lesbian, bisexual, and otherwise same-gender-partnered pastors.

I had known this was coming. From my first days in the ELCA, I was told over and over that there was great division about "gay ordination." I'd sat through sexuality study after sexuality study, learning even more ways to contextualize the "clobber verses" and simultaneously learning that there was no level of historical or philosophical argument that would convince a seeming majority of the church I had been called to serve. "The Bible said it; I believe it; that settles it." While in college, I was continually championed in my pursuit of ministry. I was given more and more leadership roles, first as a coleader of the Progressive Christian Fellowship, then as president of the campus chapel and chaplain to the Saint Olaf Choir. Over and over my classmates recognized my call to service and rewarded it with more work (which I loved). I took on too much and burned out, then bounced back again. My faith and convictions surged through me; my prayers were fervent and daily; my hopes were high. I was affirmed, again and again.

But at the same time my professors and campus pastors warned me: college was not like the real world. "You should have a backup plan," they murmured when I talked about seminary. They were happy to write letters of recommendation and make suggestions about the best Lutheran schools, but each conversation ended the same way: "I really hope there is a place for you, but you need to know there may not be." I knew what the real world was; in the age before everyone had a blog, I was writing passionate letters to the editors of local and national Lutheran publications, demanding my voice be heard among the "scholars" who had found yet more proof for the success of conversion therapy. But I believed those kinds of people lived somewhere else. They weren't here in Minnesota; they were off in Montana or South Carolina or Nevada. They weren't going to be my seminary professors, and they certainly wouldn't be my classmates.

I discovered in the back of that faculty van that I was wrong.

I felt my fingernails biting into the palm of my hand; I was methodically clenching my fist without realizing it. I did not look at him. When my introduction came, I mentioned my girlfriend, staring out the front windshield, my self-protective rage dulling anything approaching openness or friendliness. No one responded, and we moved on to the next introduction. I didn't look around the van to see if anyone was on my side; I didn't want to know. I was quiet at dinner. I hopped a bus back to my apartment instead of riding back to campus in the van. I didn't want to see yet more evidence that all the warnings of the past years were coming true: I was not going to be accepted here.

At least I'd been well equipped. At age twenty-five, I had nine years' experience of defending myself against Christianized homophobia. My life was a walking answer to "How *do* you reconcile your sexuality with the Bible?"

My best answer was that the Scriptures had nothing to say on same-gender relationships. The Bible couldn't speak on queer people in the same way that we could not ask it about best practices for automotive design; the information simply wasn't there. The writers of the Scriptures had no working concept of sexual orientation or gender identity, nor did their interpreters for the next eighteen hundred years. Even the instructions for heterosexuality were ragingly outdated; women have the right to initiate divorce now, for example. And who was going to keep track of who sat in what chair during what time of the month?[1] The Bible was a collection of our faith ancestors' best attempts to describe their encounters with the divine, but just as we were hindered by our own time and place, so were they. The culture was just too far away for us to derive anything meaningful from it, not without a significant amount of context, and even then all that we knew should always be questioned.

This was the interpretation I rested in for years. It protected me from the spiritual violence dealt upon my fellow queer family; it resonated with my understandings of feminist critiques of the texts. It wasn't impossible to still find meaning in the Bible; it was like a museum piece, one that still confessed to realities about humanity and, if investigated well enough, to how that humanity had once experienced God. There was enough in religious practice—worship, prayer, fellowship—to keep me grounded even when Bible study set my teeth on edge. I developed a spiritual allergy to words like *inspired*. I felt anxious and itchy around people who talked about "their walk with the Lord" or who came to worship carrying heavily highlighted Bibles. As a seminarian and then an intern pastor, this distrust was a constant companion.

In my feminist theologies class, I was finally given a name for my distrust: *a hermeneutic of suspicion*. Built on the work of Paul Ricoeur, it captured the modernist practice of distrusting self-proclaimed truths and looking instead for omissions and inconsistencies. In feminist theologies, it meant an awareness of the patriarchal and misogynist societies in which the Scriptures were written and formed, and a continual open identification of where women and other minority voices had been silenced. A hermeneutic of suspicion went even beyond the historical context of Scripture and began to ask: what *doesn't* the story tell us?

In theologies from the margins, especially those informed by trauma, I found writers who spoke my language. As I had as a child, it was in books that I found myself reflected. The women who had gone before me in service to the church understood what it was like to have a constant battle with the text, to be both drawn to it and tormented by it, to be captured by the story of Jesus only to be beaten by the men who wielded it. Rita Nakashima Brock and Rebecca Parker gently but firmly took apart theologies that glorified suffering. These teachings, many of them seemingly rooted in the redemptive suffering of Jesus on the cross, had been used to downplay sexual assault and force people (mostly women) to stay in abusive relationships. Brock and Parker refused to let the church—and God—off the hook. Alongside them I read James Cone, who declared that Jesus's death had political, religious, and racial motives—just as the lynching of black bodies had in America. The death of Jesus had cosmic implications, to be sure, but also embodied an earthly story of divine solidarity with the oppressed. In this story I heard the echoes of Holy Week, of a Jesus who knew the consequences of his message and yet would not—in the end, even in death could not—be silenced.

From Cone I was led to Gustavo Gutiérrez and liberation theology, the story of what it meant for God to take the side of the poor. God was a God not only of spiritual salvation but of earthly freedom, of liberation from unjust systems that relied on economic disparity. To ignore the suffering of the neighbor in the pursuit of wealth and power was an unabashed affront to the prophets and rejection of the kingdom of God. Gutiérrez then delivered me to a new liberation theologian: Marcella Althaus-Reid. Althaus-Reid was the first writer I encountered who took conversations of sexuality, sexual orientation, and gender identity beyond the six or eight "clobber verses" I had learned to shield myself from.

These were not voices found in the traditional curriculum. I had to find them in nonrequired classes, opt in to professors who were not white male Americans. These voices did not all agree with each other and certainly were not the darlings of "traditional" theologians. They were radical, they were offensive, they were trouble. I liked them.

Suddenly the whole of Scripture was open to me again through what was termed *queer theology*. Informed by queer theory, these theologians had begun to push at the edges of Scripture, employing a hermeneutic of suspicion to unravel the apparent silence around non-cisheteronormative sexuality. Queer theology took seriously the religious trauma of LGBTQ+ people and refused to let it continue unquestioned. It found space in biblical culture and even within the Scripture stories for those who did not "conform." It ceased splitting the non-cisheterosexual community into smaller and smaller identities but bound us together, calling us to advocate for each other. Through queer theology, I began to relearn queer history: the trans women of color who had refused to back down at Stonewall; the lesbians who had cared for the gay men dying in rapid succession from the AIDS epidemic our president would not recognize; the criminalization of sex work that simultaneously fetishized teens, people of color, and nonbinary identities.

Far more than *gay* had been, *queer* was the key to unlock my world. My differences from others were not restricted to the body I was born in or the gender of those I fell in love with. That was perhaps where the separation began, but because of it, I had questions not only about gender and sex but about religion, politics, philosophy, psychology. The answers that seemingly worked for everyone else did not work for me. I was coming to understand that in me intersected a variety of blessings and curses, privileges and oppressions: white and cis and upper-middle-class, female and gay. *Queer* reminded me daily that those collisions of identity had to be resolved, that I was not an individual but a part of a community that commonly experienced bigotry, oppression, isolation, and violence. The best vision of that community made space for the other marginalized voices, bringing them together in a jarring but interwoven harmony: God was not just for the individual but for the salvation and transformation of the whole community. In choosing to be made flesh among the poor, the downtrodden, the minority, the sexually suspect, God had declared divine unity with us.

Finally, there were voices putting words to my long-fought struggles with the Scriptures. I was no longer alone in my fear. I had ancestors in the faith, wiser and kinder than me, who had gone before into the wilderness and come back alive and stronger. I needed this, the model of those who had stared down the Bible and survived. The word *suspicion* had begun to fall short for me. It had come from a straight white man summarizing the modernist tendencies of other straight white men (namely Freud, Marx, and Nietzsche). Suspicion seemed like a philosophical hobby for those so burdened by their own privilege and genius they had to find *something* to occupy their time. This was not a parlor game for me, a murder mystery to page through warm by the fireside. This was, as Rev. Broderick Greer would name it, a hermeneutic of survival. I had to find a way to cope with the violence of Scripture, both what was literally contained within its pages and how it had been used to wound over two thousand years of cultural domination. I would not be able to exist within the church if I could not find a way to read the stories of its faith.

For years all I could do was cling to the best story I could find—a nightmare.

In the days after the resurrection of Jesus, Peter—the Rock, the one who sank like a stone, the one as thick as a box of rocks—was staying in the town of Joppa. He was hungry, and while lunch was being prepared he went up to the roof to pray. He "fell into a trance" (or, perhaps, was faint with hunger) and saw a vision: a sheet, dropping down from heaven, full of every unclean animal one could imagine. Eagles and snakes, bats and camels, lobsters and pigs. Peter's growling stomach turned over in disgust. And a voice from heaven said, "Get up, Peter. Kill and eat."[2]

The image was beyond nauseating. Peter was a preacher of the good news of Jesus of Nazareth, one of the Twelve.

He had been taught religious dietary laws since he was old enough to chew.[3] Those laws were one of the central ways of affirming his part in the chosen people of God. How could he violate God's laws?

This was no ordinary nightmare. It was a vision from the Holy Spirit to prepare him for the arrival of Cornelius's messengers. A Roman centurion, "a devout man who feared God," had been told by an angel to send for Peter. Peter invited Cornelius's messengers into his home (which, according to stricter interpretations of religious law, could have compromised the ritual purity of his house). Peter then returned with them to Cornelius's home, where he proclaimed the good news of Jesus and baptized his whole household—the second gentile converts into what until then had been an entirely Jewish sect. Peter promised, "I truly understand that God shows no partiality," but the news apparently had not reached the Jewish Christians in Jerusalem, who demanded an account of his actions. Sure, there were prophecies throughout the Hebrew Scriptures of a global reconciliation where all nations came to Jerusalem for healing and new life—but like this? With no circumcision, no dietary laws, no conversion to Judaism first? The letter of the law demanded otherwise, but Peter remained convicted: "we will be saved through the Lord Jesus, just as they will."[4]

Perhaps this was a guide for the church today. Just as Peter had been willing to move beyond everything he'd known in order to follow the Spirit, perhaps the church would be willing to give up on its legalistic interpretation of Leviticus to welcome me in—just as I was.

I stayed in the Gospels and the Acts of the Apostles as often as I could, focusing there for preaching and Bible study and essay metaphors. There, I could join with Jesus in an ire toward the religious elite and both a respect for the Scripture of history but an awareness that its legalistic application could mean further harm or death for those who were already in distress. *You tithe mint and dill and cumin, but neglect the weightier matters of the law: justice and mercy and faith!*[5] The prophets could be safe, especially the justice-oriented books like Amos and Micah, but if I was not careful enough I'd find myself in the whore language of Ezekiel and, once again, have to shield myself with Hebrew grammar books and historical-critical critiques until I could find a way out of the battle and into safety—which was usually anything in the category of "not the Bible."

I was a good enough writer and preacher, especially if the Scripture in question was from the Gospels, to make up for my survival mechanisms. I did my best to hide my fear of the Bible. Some of it was respect for others; I didn't want to burden those who had no issue with it. But just as much (or more) was my own exhaustion. I was tired. I was tired of explaining myself to everyone. I was tired of feeling my walls shoot up in every conversation, tired of distrusting every new acquaintance who showed a little too much interest in my religious beliefs. I was tired of lying awake at night coming up with new and multilayered metaphors for explaining how I could reconcile the "clear voice" of Scripture with my "lifestyle choice." I was just tired. It was easier to pretend that Scripture and I had a happy marriage where all our concerns had long ago been resolved and we were now working together in perfect harmony toward a better proclamation of the good news throughout the world.

And then it all unraveled under the weight of fourteen words.

It was 2013. I was one year into my two-year internship and still taking courses part-time. My internship church supervisor (and their solo pastor) had been called to a new role, which left me carrying a larger burden than I'd expected when an interim pastor began serving. Most of my friends had completed their internships and would be returning for senior year in the fall, but they weren't planning to be residential students—they were getting married, having babies, buying houses, and settling down. Meanwhile, I was living in a friend's basement in the suburbs, drawing from savings to pay rent and stretch my meager monthly stipend.

In summary: most of my world, in the six months prior, had gone absolutely opposite of my plans, and I was a prime candidate for losing my grip on anything else.

It was a simple quote out of a lecture at the Festival of Homiletics, by author and theologian Dr. Lauren Winner:

"What if our job as preachers is to just love the Scriptures in public?"

And I felt my heart crack down the middle. "Loving the Scriptures" was an impossibility. The Scriptures were a receptacle for every queer- and transphobic, misogynist, white supremacist, and otherwise power-hungry excuse for violence and destruction over the past two thousand years. I could dig a gold nugget out of that pile of rubbish if I worked hard enough, but I was never going to *love* it. No one could love a weapon that has beaten their family black and blue.

I carried my self-protective anger for days. Who did this Dr. Winner think she was? She might have escaped the ravages of "Christian" practice to be able to claim this vile "love" for the Scriptures, but imposing it on others was just doubling down on the cruelty. Yet another sign of the violence inherent in the system.

I was angry because I knew she was right. I knew that I was burning out. Others lived and even flourished with the hermeneutic of suspicion, but it was eating me alive. My self-protective shield against Scripture had turned into a burden I could not carry. I had been working full time for ten years to put my life into ministry, to testify to the presence of *some* sort of truth and reality in Scripture, despite the fact that I didn't believe in its literal King James perfection. I needed more than suspicion. I needed more than survival. I felt bitingly jealous of those who did not.

I did not have a plan for how I would accomplish falling in love with Scripture. I simply decided that I had to and went from there. I bought a new Bible—New Revised Standard Version, the size of a hymnal, with no study notes or margins to speak of. This was not a scholastic project. This was not about worship or preaching. This was about falling in love.

I started on page one and just kept going. I was on a schedule; I had to get through the whole of the Bible in ninety days, which meant about sixteen chapters a day. There was not enough time for in-depth consideration of the Hebrew or a deep scholarly dive on each verse. Some days I would have to go through multiple books at once. If an idea struck while reading, I had about five words' worth of space to make note of it. If something resounded with me, I highlighted it. And I just kept going, sixteen chapters a day, ninety days in a row.

I treated the Bible like I treated *Harry Potter* or *Buffy the Vampire Slayer* or *Star Wars* or any other story with multiple volumes and characters I loved. It was made by humans. There would be mistakes. But the creators were trying to convey something beautiful, something important, something true, and if I could believe in good intent on their part, I could believe it for the authors of the Scriptures as well.

Three days in, I found the story that would come to guide my new relationship with the Scriptures: the story of Jacob and the man who wrestled with him. Having stolen his brother Esau's birthright and blessing, Jacob served his uncle Laban for twenty years, but he caused enough trouble for himself there that he decided to return home. He sent messengers ahead to his brother, who then came out to meet him with four hundred men—an army, Jacob was sure, that would overtake him and his wives and children and destroy them for the injustice done to Esau. Jacob prayed desperately for God's protection and then sent an enormous flock of goats and sheep and camels and cows ahead of him, hoping for his brother's mercy. He then sent his wives and concubines and children across the river and stayed by himself for a sleepless night.[6]

A man appeared—no description, no buildup, only the sudden existence of an *enosh* who wrestled Jacob all night until dawn. The man could not beat Jacob—in many interpretations of the story that meant Jacob was winning—and so he struck Jacob on the hip, crippling him permanently. Even still Jacob persevered, pinning the man: "I will not let you go unless you bless me." *Fine*, said the stranger. *Here's your blessing: you are no longer Jacob, heel-grabber, trickster, one who takes what is not his own. You are now Yisra-El, for you have striven with both God and with humanity, and you have prevailed.* Jacob—no, Israel—would never walk properly again; but neither would he be the man who had stolen his brother's life and incurred Esau's murderous wrath. When daylight came and Esau arrived, he fell on his brother Jacob-Israel's neck, weeping with joy to see him again.[7]

I knew the dread that Jacob had felt. I knew what it was like to abandon what I had known for a new land. I refused the binary offered me of choosing either my faith or my sexuality, loving Jesus or loving my future wife. I had made a new way for myself, in college and seminary, finding my own voice and claiming my own gifts. Each time I opened the Scriptures I felt a raw fear, like I was staring down my own destruction. I was going to have to make peace with this, with Scripture, with a holy book that would be used over and over again to wound me and my queer family.

Some days the Scripture I read would eat at me until nightfall. Some nights were sleepless or restless. I knew what the psalmist had wrung from the depths of their heart: *I am weary with my moaning; every night I flood my bed with tears.*[8] I kept going. I kept reading and tossing and turning. When Scripture kept me up, I stayed up with it, unwilling to quit, exhausted but still holding on. I felt the wounds again, the thousands of years of abuse that Scripture had been twisted to encourage. My heart beat with a limp. I still would not give up. *I will not let you go unless you bless me*, I whispered again and again. There was a blessing in the story—I had to believe this—and if I had to pin it down and sit on it until it cried uncle, I would do it. I would wait for the dawn, for Scripture to look me in the eye and say: *You are not what everyone else says about you.* And I would wait and trust that one day, the enemy that was the church would embrace me, falling on my neck and weeping with joy at our reunion.

I would come to call this way of reading *the hermeneutic of the hip.* The fall after I completed my ninety-day journey, I came across an essay by Phyllis Trible:

> Jacob's defiant words to the stranger I take as a challenge to the Bible itself: "I will not let you go unless you bless me." I will not let go of the book unless it blesses me. I will struggle with it. I will not turn it over to my enemies that it curse me. Neither will I turn over to friends who wish to curse it. No, over against the cursing from either Bible-thumpers or Bible-bashers, I shall hold fast for blessing. But I am under no illusion that blessing, if it comes, will be on my terms—that I will not be changed in the process. . . . The storyteller reports: "The sun rose upon

him [Jacob] . . . limping because of his hip." Through this ancient story, appropriated anew, Biblical studies, faith and feminism converge for me. Wrestling with the words, to the light I limp.[9]

This was a metaphor that could sustain me. It took me beyond suspicion or survival. It looked beyond "wrestling with the text." It recognized the danger in every time I opened the Scriptures, every new encounter with a fellow Christian, every brutal beating that had been given in God's name throughout history. This story affirmed wrestling and its results—it reminded me why I trusted those best who were unafraid to name their own strugglings with the Scriptures and the church. We have diverse causes, a variety of experiences, each our own individual traumas, and yet in our many ways we bear a similar scar, a joint out of place, a blessing with a new name that saw our striving and called it wrestling with God. My family on the margins—queer and trans, but also women, people of color, the disabled, the poor and hungry, the refugee and outcast, my fellow sufferers of mental illness—has known what it is like to wake up day by day in a life that challenges the easy promises of American Christianity, a life that lived even to its best can never overcome the adversity laid before us simply by "trying harder." We know the truth: sometimes coming face to face with God sends us away bruised and yet blessed.

Some of us walk away forever. There is too much wounding. I carry with me many stories of those who have found no more blessing in the struggle. The church, the Scriptures, God are all too wounding still. It is my responsibility—and, I believe, the church's—to bear these stories, to witness to them and face unafraid the truth of what has been done in the supposed name of God. We are to honor these stories. To fear and silence them is to ignore the presence of God, who meets us not just in glory but also in suffering, who to give a blessing did not pronounce it from rendered heavens but whispered out a new name, pinned in the dark before the dawn.

In that whisper I hear not just God's blessing for us who wrestle but a recognition of the strength and stubbornness in our own persistence. There is no promise of safety, since such a promise would be a lie; the faith enshrined in Scripture has rarely been a miraculous preventative against sickness, suffering, or death. But there is a promise of transformation, a change from our past to a future with our strivings not held against us but honored. There is a promise of dawn, of shadow giving way to sunshine, of a new day with no mistakes yet in it and the chance to claim again for ourselves our own healing and peace. And there is a promise of miracles: an estranged brother with his arms around our neck, weeping for joy that we have returned, our long-fought battles with self and God and others turned into a lasting welcome home.

CHAPTER 7

SHUT UP

In my second year of seminary, I stopped speaking of God.

A year before, in the quick succession of twenty days, six different gay teen boys across America took their own lives. For a few short weeks, the torment of being young and gay in America dominated the national conversation. Organizations sprung up to flood social media with videos promising "It Gets Better"; funding and donations increased for suicide hotlines. Some progressive churches rushed to publish their own statements of affirmation and promises for a brighter future, but most "faith-based" organizations shrugged, folded their hands, and waited it out. Exodus International, the long-running and largest organization offering Christian conversion therapy, cancelled its yearly "Day of Truth" out of respect for the dead; Focus on the Family picked it up and turned it into the "Day of Dialogue." They were bold enough to admit they believed that, despite the epidemic of self-destruction, it was still crucial that America know "God's design for sexuality."

That summer, I had done my chaplaincy rotation, as required of all future ELCA pastors: four hundred hours in a hospital or other clinical setting that offered spiritual care. I watched men younger than my father wasting away from the same illnesses that were, at home, ravaging his body. I sat for hours with patients stricken with Alzheimer's and dementia, minds locked inside bodies that could not coordinate. I talked to a schizophrenic who told me the world was divided into Cains and Abels, and there was nothing that could be done to save the Cains. (Not all religious opinions, no matter how firmly held, are accurate representations of the Bible *or* of reality.)

I held the hand of a woman so jaundiced from alcoholic liver failure that her skin was highlighter-yellow and who talked in hushed tones with her children and grandchildren about apologies and forgiveness and resentment and why "rock bottom" didn't come sooner than "certain death." I sat in rooms with eating-disorder patients, some younger than twelve, some older than my mother; some of them had come desperate for help, weakening hands clinging to whatever might free them, while others had been brought by families numb from exhaustion, their compassion and cooperation drying up. I sat by the bedside of seventy-two-hour psych-holds fighting years of depression, isolation, drug use, and suicidal ideation.

I was tired of talking of God. It was an exercise in futility. I did not want to talk about the sixth-century formation of the Benedictine monastic societies. I *definitely* did not want to talk about Paul's vocabulary and grammatical structures and how they borrowed from ancient love poetry. I didn't feel like reading the Gospels or preaching anything about anyone, least of all God. The world was in crisis; my queer family was tearing itself from the world child by child. All I saw, in the words upon words about God that I was asked to read and write and regurgitate into essays and exams, was philosophical babble that had, at best, stopped caring about application and practice and, more often, was fully culpable in the systems that had contributed to the suffering and death around me.

The more I was offered the chance to explore the myriad of ways the people of God had accounted for the inner life of the divine, the less I felt connected to the reality of pain around me. The churches that shoved me to the side for my gender or my sexuality were not interested in my academic understanding of medieval philosophy's influence on Aquinas's *via antiqua*. The God of my Christian ancestors might have been rich in interpretation, but the God of American religion was distant, domineering, destructive—and male.

I saw God clothed in skin God never knew: lily-white, pure as snow. I saw that the God of America could not be the God of a black Democratic president; God could only be the God of the Republican party, the party that had freed the slaves and thus solved all of racism forever and ever amen. The God who had brought the Israelite children out of slavery in Egypt in a pillar of cloud by day and a pillar of fire by night was coming to look far more like the Romans who killed the Son than the Hebrews who had borne him.

I saw God used to throw aside science, to ignore the cries of creation, to stifle the shouts of the oppressed. I heard that God was a God not of what is but only of what is to come. The American church proclaimed that faith was a self-alignment with right doctrine, a confession that switched the eternal railroad track from hell to heaven but made no alterations in the journey here on earth—except to spread the truth of the God who was not interested in the pains of this world, only the number of souls that would make it to the next.

I saw God used to manipulate and destroy. I heard that God was a God of righteousness, of expectations, of swift vengeance. This God would not tolerate insubordination. Those who fell short, who were too bound by their temptations and failed to claim the truth of the divine, would burn forever. Those who could not obtain and preserve their own purity were already forsaken. God hated the sin of the world, found my broken self abhorrent, and had to sacrifice his one and only Son to spare me from the hell I most assuredly deserved.

I saw God used to sanction the actions of men. I heard that God was trampling out the blood of the conquered, not only masculine but dominant, militant, eternally victorious. The American church promised that God would dress us in holy armor and guarantee the conquest of our enemies. Pastor after pastor insisted that God was male, of course, and male had been made first; the primacy of men was not only cultural but divinely sanctioned, and patriarchy was not only the way it had always been but the way it would always be. Professors forcibly demanded our right confession that God was domineering, God's grace irresistible: once God had chosen you, you had no say in the matter.

I saw God turned from a source of love to the reason for hate.

I tried to talk of an inclusive vision of God, of tugging at the boundaries of the word until they were big enough to hold the divine. My friends and I worked together on a student-led project for inclusive and expansive language, trying to explain to our professors and peers where "God" was falling short for us. *Maybe less with the masculine pronouns*, we said. *Maybe God is a pronoun in and of itself? Maybe, in the face of sexual assault and rape culture, we reconsider speaking of God as violent and unrelenting?* But not much changed, and after a while, I would not speak of God anymore.

This is an inconvenient position in seminary. This is an inconvenient position for a future pastor. But more than anything, it was impossible—because even as I was loath to speak of God, I loved speaking of God.

I remembered the words of Jeremiah: *If I say I will not mention the Lord, or speak any more in God's name, then within me there is something like a burning fire shut up in my bones.*[1] I did not love to speak of the domineering and distant God, who meted out judgments from His throne on high. That God had no goodness for me. But that same word *God* that soured in my mouth in class and mocked me in every paper was the God who met me in the Scriptures, a God I needed and craved. That God, the real God, stood in stark contrast to all the offerings of the religion that devoured the people on the margins of life. That was a God I could curl into, like a cat on a blanket; a God who wrapped around my shoulders like the scent of lilies in an all-night meditation garden.

The God of the Scriptures came close enough to touch the earth. At the beginning of it all, the spirit of God was a wind that soared over the deep, a breath that stirred the waters into waves. God knelt in the dust and knit together a creature made of earth—the creature who would become our ancestor, we broken and beautiful creatures made of the same stuff as dust and stardust. Again and again God appeared: a voice, a messenger, a promise, a promise to us who had wandered away or been chased off. When Joseph cried out in prison, God was close enough to hear. When the people cried out in slavery, God was close enough to act. God turned water into blood and dust into gnats and nothingness into frogs until the weight of God's call for freedom hung in the air like death and Pharaoh said *Get out. Get out, and don't come back.* And again a wind moved over the waters, and again dry land appeared.[2]

God stayed close, too immense to be held and yet too loving to be gone. The God of the Scriptures pleaded until the divine voice cracked, begging our ancestors in the wilderness: *I brought you out of slavery. Don't chain yourself to other gods who will drain you dry. Don't claim the reckless power of Egypt for yourselves, crushing your neighbor beneath the weight of your own supposed magnificence. I set you free. Try to stay there.* Time and time again our cruelty cracked God's heart, and time and time again God would not go. God had not set the world in motion only to disappear to the far reaches of the cosmos.

God's voice still breathed through the wind, calling the judges and prophets, delivering David only to find that he, too, was human, and sending Nathan to call him to account. There was nowhere, the psalmists found, that God could not be found too—not even in the seeming endless dark.[3]

The God of the Scriptures, in fact, has met us clothed in darkness. God appeared not in a glorious golden tearing of heaven's snow-white clouds but in startling places, fiery and dirty and shadowed. God burst into flame in the middle of a desert, an echoing voice from everywhere and nowhere: *I Am Who I Am.* God hid in cloud and lightning. God spoke through the Hebrew judges and prophets, through Deborah under her palm tree, through the shouts of the prophets and the shaking voice of Mordecai: *Perhaps you were made for such a time as this.*[4]

God has met us clothed in weakness. God stood on the side of the underdog, the minority, the slave, the oppressed. God cried out in the devastated voices of the prophets: *The oppressed! The widow! The orphan! How have you gone so long and so far away from what it means to love the least?* God closed the divine eyes and whispered a promise: the servant of God would be so tender that a bruised reed would not break under his feet, nor a dim wick be snuffed out by his hand.[5]

God put on skin and walked among us, no less than perfectly human and yet so much more, his feet dusty with Judea's sand, his cheeks a shining reflection of the desert's heat. God cracked open the sky and poured down in a wind so strange it looked like the shape of a dove. When the Romans came to arrest him, he was indistinguishable from the Jews around him and could only be betrayed with a kiss. When God died, the sky turned black and the curtain of the temple tore down the center. The body of God, forehead and feet, eyes and elbows, dreaded hair all wound up with dust and sweat and suffering— the flesh that had held the divine was empty, wrapped, hastily buried in a borrowed tomb.[6]

And then God was up again, out in the world, untamed and uncontrollable. God walked through walls and cooked fish and held out wrists and feet still marred by nails.[7] Resurrection had not taken away the pain, the wounds, the vulnerability. It had transformed them from death into new life. That was how Love had defeated Death; not in domination but in transformation. God was real, scarred, human—no lily-white perfection. This was no conquering force, no marching army. This was love at its finest and rarest and most raw.

This was a scrabbly God, gleaning what was dropped, picking the losing side every time. This was a brown God, dressing in skin rich and dark. This was a God who worked not with a commanding voice but in a whisper that was best heard in sheer silence, a God who was joyfully stuck with whoever was willing to say "yes." This was a God who relied on "yes," who sent an angel with six eyes lowered in reverence to sing: *Greetings, favored one. The Lord is with you.*[8]

The God of the Scriptures, in fact, relied on women.

There were two stories of how the world had come to be. In the first, God was there and there was nothing but a watery globe; then suddenly light and dark, sky and sea, land and water, sun and moon—for this was not a God who did things in order—fish and birds and beasts of the earth, and then, at the closing dusk of the sixth day, a thing made in God's image, male and female, as widely diverse as the night and day that had come before them.⁹ Women were there at the first, to relish in the day of rest, to learn to work the earth and care for it.

In the second story, before the rain, before the plants, there was Ha'adam, the creature made of dust. Strong enough to till the earth, gentle enough to sow the seeds, but lonely, without a helper, all alone in the garden of Eden. And so God made animals—cows and goats, sparrows and owls, quail and lizards and foxes and pigs, turtles and lions and elephants—but none of them were a suitable helper, a workable partner. So the dust-creature slept, and God made a second creature, pulling one rib from Ha'adam's side. Then and only then did the dust-creature say: "This is Woman, for out of Man she was taken"; then and only then, when the Woman had appeared, was creation complete.¹⁰

The God of the Scriptures needed women. We bore every generation that called upon the God of Abraham and Isaac and Jacob. Men ran roughshod over us, used us until we were no longer of use, and sent us into the wilderness to starve. But God was not far behind. Hagar, tucking her son Ishmael under a bush to die, found that the God-who-sees had seen her again.¹¹ These were no wilting-desert-flower women. They cooked the meals and told the stories; they found their way despite impossibilities. They were the ones who put Moses into the water, who watched him, who fished him out and cared for him.[12] They were the outsiders who, through cleverness and confession and hard work, made their way in: Rahab with her red cord, Ruth with her barley sack.[13] The God of the Scriptures saw these women—the mothers and the widows and the slaves and the sex workers, all my ancestors on the edges of acceptable society—and brought us in, expanding the circle of the people of God.

God-in-flesh needed women. The spirit that had blown over the face of the waters now came to rest in the waters of Mary's womb, and a new chapter in God's life had begun. God knew that teenage girls and unwed mothers are some of the strongest forces on earth. God learned to walk in human feet with women's hands catching him. We women surrounded him in ministry, housed him when no one else had room, cooked for twelve or more, found the funds to keep the mission going. We women were there at the cross, to witness the final cries of God when all the devoted disciples had fled, and women were there at the tomb that dewy morning, when the light of dawn shone like the first day of creation. *How impossible*, the women thought, *that the sun could go on rising, when all hope is dead.* "How impossible," the men laughed, hours later, "such an idle tale, women's gossip! How could anyone be raised from the dead?"[14]

God-in-flesh needed women, even if the men failed to notice. And when they had waited long enough, God blew through the room with the same wind that soared over the face of the deep before creation; lit foreheads with the same flicker of flame that had called out to Moses; sent them out, one by one: *Time to fly from the nest, little birds. Tell of what you know.*[15]

The God of the Scriptures knew what it was like to fly. If God had a mighty arm to deliver the Israelites from slavery and feet that rested on earth like a footstool, God too had wide-spreading wings. Moses sung of how God had soared on them, carrying the children of Israel: *like an eagle that stirs up its nest and carries them.* The psalmists had found comfort there: *Hide me in the shadow of your wings.* God-in-flesh had stood before the holy city of Jerusalem and wept: *How I have longed to gather you under my wings, as a hen gathers up her chicks.*[16]

God's tenderness began to enfold me, like a child curling into her mother's lap. I resisted the lies of the God of American religion and clung instead to the God of a world far away and yet so much closer than the false idols of power and perfection. Each night my failures soaked my sheets in tears; each day I felt I could not face, I remembered the impossible promises: *You are my child*, God had said to Israel—and to me. *You are beloved*, God had said to Jesus—and to me. *I am with you always*, Jesus had said to the disciples—and to me.[17] I knew a God who was controlling and made demands was far more palatable. I knew the world preferred a God who snatched away salvation when the scales of sin were tipped just far enough. That was a God the church could control; that was a God that power could wield against those who could not fight back. I tried to breathe into the possibility that God was bigger than that, was more wily and less inclined to scorekeeping. I tried to trust that the unknown prophet, surrounded by the ruined walls of Jerusalem, laden with bitterness and swallowed up in grief, both a sinner and broken by the sin of others, had told the best of truth: *The steadfast love of the Lord never ceases, God's mercies never come to an end; they are new every morning; great is the faithfulness of God.*[18]

Among the prophets I found more promise. They proclaimed a God of judgment, yes, and I felt my shoulders curl in self-protection; but the longer I read, the more I found they proclaimed a God of judgment not against the minority on the edge but against the powers of their day. The prophets knew what it was like to preach against the tide, to be crying out for redemption and find their voices drowned by the religious elite who promised peace when there was no peace. I had once thought I was meant to fear this warrior God, unsheathing a sword against me, the enemy; now I began to wonder if I was the one to be defended. What if it was God who stood against those who would condemn me? Then I was not alone but strengthened, helped, upheld with the victorious hand of the divine. Then it was not just to Israel and Jacob but to *me* that God said: *You are precious in my sight, and honored, and I love you; do not be afraid, for I am with you—I have called you by name, and you are mine.*[19]

I saw among my family on the edges how desperately we need the proclamation of a God not of dominating empire but of intimate compassion, not a God of might but of mercy. I began to see that every time I felt alone, in reality I had my hands on a long and well-worn rope, pulling me and mine back to the God confessed in the witness of the Scriptures.

In the prophets, we find a God whose warrior might is inextricable from tender compassion. Encountering the lost and forgotten, God drops the divine shield and instead weeps like a woman in labor, crying out with birthing pains. There was no better metaphor for God's struggle, God's pain, God's desire for us than to imagine her as a woman, on the edge of becoming a mother, kneeling in sweat and tears and blood to bring us forth into new life. This woman God was clearing out the wilderness, sweeping out the desert, opening up the impossible places to make a way for all to come near. All the scattered would be gathered, all the weary welcomed home. We might feel that God had forgotten us, here on the edge of the world, but she called back across the miles: *Can a woman forget her nursing child, or show no compassion for the babe of her womb? No matter how far away you go, I will be there to welcome you home. Look—you are part of me, too; you are tattooed on the palms of my hands.*[20]

In the moments when the church stood to exclude me, I rested in the arms of a woman warrior God. In the moments when my privilege or my brokenness tempted me with power and disinterest, God stood beside me to break the walls of division. God was both powerful and capable, strong enough to deal out retribution and skilled enough to deliver a child. The mothering God shouted in an uproar against those who rejected others "for the sake of the Lord" and then knelt by the side of Zion like a midwife easing new life into the world.[21] The mother God held me, calmed and quieted my soul when I was troubled. For a while I rested in the arms of this mother

God; the father-figure of the Scriptures was still too fierce to come near.

But this was not enough. I wanted to untangle God the Father from God the Crucifier, the judge from far off whose nose curled in revulsion at my sin. I wanted to know the God who did not believe in overpowering the world but in dying in it. I wanted to find God the Father in God the Crucified. There was where God was known best, Martin Luther had said—in suffering and death, in Love incarnate nailed to rough-hewn wood. I thought of Jesus, not a week before his own death, standing outside the tomb of his dear friend: *Lazarus, come out!* I wanted to know the God who was not tied up in death, the God who was not wrapped in the clothes of power and patriarchy. I listened for the voice of Jesus: *Unbind him. Let him go.*[22]

I began to know the tenderness of God, seen through God-in-flesh's eyes. I saw the fathering God that Jesus knew at twelve, the Master of the Universe whose house was where his son could call home. I saw the fathering God who called for love, even in the face of hate—who sent rain on the just and unjust, who was merciful beyond perfection, who offered that mercy to his children not as an end but as an inheritance to offer to others. I breathed into that mercy, let it flow through me with power not of my own perfection but of my endless chance at a new start. I heard of the fathering God who hid revelation from the wise and powerful, and offered it to children and the unimportant, and with the disciples I wondered at a God who was willing to waste such revelation on me.[23]

I knelt with wonder at the feet of a fathering God whose name was meant to be precious, to be used with care and compassion, as all things hallowed should be. I heard of the fathering God's kingdom to come, a kingdom not of this world but of a place where might and right were no match for mercy and redemption. I wondered at a fathering God who wanted to feed his children, to care for their needs, to release them from the bonds of both their own sin and the sins of others, who longed to protect them from times of suffering and trial. When those times came, when suffering was near at hand and sweat was thick as drops of blood, I knew the promise of a fathering God who did not release and yet could not abandon. When the world thirsted to turn against me, to see my body bent and my spirit broken—when church leaders insisted on a fathering God who was vindictive and violent, I clung to the words of the cross: *Father, forgive them, for they know not what they do. Into your hands I commend my spirit.*[24]

Like the wind over the waters at creation, the fathering God came close to me, unsettling my calm. I returned to the stories, working my fingers into them like fibers in a loom, unwilling to let go of the God of the Scriptures for the easier God of masculinity and might. *There was a man who had two sons*, I whispered.[25] There were days I knew what it was to be the younger son: to have hated where I came from, to have taken whatever I could grab and run away, to have found myself penniless and worthless in a land where no one cared about my hunger. There were days I knew what it was to be the older son, the diligent one, staying close to the father's side, infuriated by the upstart younger brother who thought he knew so much better to take off with a third of the family's wealth before it was his to own. On all the days I kept hoping in a God who was like that father, who threw a party for the son who returned and who invited in the son that had never left: *Rejoice with me.*

Rejoice with me, God-in-flesh said, telling the story of a father, and the fathering God who saw in secret welcomed us home in celebration.

Rejoice with me, God-in-flesh said, telling the story of a shepherd, and the Good Shepherd became the story that told us who we were.

But I had forgotten the middle story. *What woman*, said God-in-flesh, *having ten silver coins and losing one . . .*

I had been found.

CHAPTER 8

UNKNOWN

But first I would have to deal with Paul.

American Christianity regards Paul as the central interpreter of the Christian faith and life. For centuries, we have turned to his words to structure our theologies and our life together. Each Sunday, it is his words we proclaim over the communion table: *On the night when Jesus was betrayed, he took bread, and when he had given thanks, he broke it and said, "This is my body, given for you. Do this in remembrance of me."*[1] It was the words of Paul that set the wheels of the Protestant Reformation turning, with Martin Luther's grand proclamation that salvation and justification rested on faith alone. From there arose Calvinism and Baptist theology and the Methodist church and the Great Awakening and nondenominationalism; most of what the white church in America looks like is derived from interpretations of the work of Paul and his epistles.

I had the fortune of being raised in the Episcopal church, who adopted some of the teachings of the Protestant Reformation but had begun the work of separatism on their own based on more political leanings. Considering my attitude toward Paul, it is a bit surprising that the Lutheran church claimed me in the end. It might have been easier to remain tied to a church that did not hinge its central philosophies on the words of a man who said that as a woman I had no right to preach and as a queer person I had no inheritance in the kingdom of God.

This is what the Holy Spirit does, it seems; I was drawn not to the logical choice but to the one compelled by theology practiced with compassion and expansion. I had been claimed by the weight of the bread in my hands, informed by a pastor who had embodied in that moment the promise of the priesthood of all believers. In the stained-glass light of a Lutheran college chapel, I felt safe enough to be vulnerable in a church again, felt reverent enough to call it holy ground. I did not know what was coming for me; I only knew I had to know more about the faith that informed this campus church that had become my home.

In my first religion course, we were to read a red paperback book by some guy named Martin Luther. The riveting historical account in the introduction explained that Luther was a sixteenth-century challenger of the Catholic Church. As a child raised in a post-Catholic home, I was already intrigued. In the assigned chapter, this Luther proclaimed:

A Christian is a perfectly free lord of all, subject to none.

A Christian is a perfectly dutiful servant of all, subject to all.

I had been spiritually wandering for years, looking for a clear explanation of the Christian life, and here it was before me: paradox. Faith was not a solution to be mastered but a mystery, a navigation between my liberation from self-righteousness and my call to care for my neighbor in need. The Scriptures were not a story to be conquered and contextualized but a promise of reality met with grace. The impossibility of it all—that God would know, from the start, how beautiful and yet broken I could be, and yet again and again offer to me forgiveness and a chance for redemption—could only make sense when wrapped in paradox. That the powerful, immortal triune God is most clearly revealed in the suffering and death of Jesus of Nazareth on the cross; that the gospel is translatable and yet unchangeable; that we are, at the core of all this, both sinner and saint simultaneously. It was a mystery, it was baffling and frustrating, and yet I knew it to be true.

But in claiming this church that was claiming me, in accepting the wide embrace of Christian faith that I was finding in Lutheran theology and practice, I would have to contend with Paul.

I knew how to take Paul apart. I had to. He remained, as I found myself dragged into Lutheranism, the perpetual thorn in my theological side. His words have been used to baptize the subjugation of the African race, the silencing of women, the systems of domestic abuse, and the persistent revulsion against queer and trans people. He is where most of my queer family quits. We can explain away Leviticus, unweave Deuteronomy, outline the history of Sodom and Gomorrah, but Paul? Paul is New Testament; Paul is New Covenant; Paul is the scriptural authority on post-resurrection Christian life, and he does not loose his bonds on us so easily.

I was taught not to be shocked by Paul's words. He was a product of his time. Women in the first century (and long before) were essentially property, handed off from father to husband, and if she outlived her husband, on to his brother or into the son's care. Opportunities for self-sufficiency were scarce; the most righteous option was to marry well like Ruth and judiciously spend her husband's wealth like Abigail. The love-song of Proverbs 31 praising a competent wife might feel more romantic if the roles the unnamed woman so graciously fills weren't the only roles women were ever offered. Women who earned their own money often did so through sex work, drawing ire and shame and condemnation. Penniless women littered the stories of the Scriptures: divorced women who had been found unfit by their husbands for any reason they liked; widowed women clutching their infant children's hands as they dropped the last of their savings into the temple box; women unclean and ostracized, struck by hemorrhaging for twelve years, beggared by the doctors who never helped. Women weren't worth the social capital it would have taken to care for them; they could not testify as a witness in court nor initiate their own divorce.[2]

Women had little to no education in the first century, especially not in logic or Scripture. Thus they were silenced in mixed-gender groups, since they were likely to ask derailing or elementary questions. Better, Paul thought, to have them ask their husbands at home, so as not to disturb worship like a six-year-old who has enjoyed the children's message so much she feels the need to participate loudly in the rest of the service as well.[3] Since men were educated and women were not, women should remain silent, and of course they could never be wise enough to teach. How could we be shocked by Paul's scathing words to women? They were uneducated and disenfranchised; he could not risk his baby churches by empowering them to speak and endangering the assembly to foolishness.

Attentive readers of Paul might notice the small problem in this analysis—namely, that Paul names and even *uplifts* the ministry of women who speak in the churches he had planted. In even the same letter, Paul sends his greetings from Aquila and Priscilla, the husband-and-wife team who had met him in Corinth and traveled with him throughout the Mediterranean. Of the six times they are mentioned in the New Testament, Priscilla (sometimes called Prisca) is named first four times. Paul would later send his great letter to the Romans by the hand of Phoebe; in the letter, he recommends her as a deacon to be welcomed "as is fitting for the saints." This reads as a typical Greco-Roman letter of recommendation, which means Phoebe not only carried the letter from Judea to Rome but *read it aloud to the assembly* when she arrived.[4] These were no silent, casserole-cooking, piano-playing, Sunday-school-only-under-the-age-of-twelve-teaching women. They were powerful; they had the right to speak and to be heard, to correct those errant in their teaching, and to be named among the many who had supported Paul in his work and been preachers of the gospel. I was reminded that Paul, like all followers of Christ, is still bound by his own time and place.

This is of little comfort to one who is prevented from preaching doubly based on Paul's words—both because of my gender and because of my sexuality. In his first letter to the Corinthians and in his first letter to Timothy, Paul confidently lists those who are "contrary to the sound teaching that conforms to the glorious gospel," who will not "inherit the kingdom of God," and in that list—among drunkards and liars, murderers and slave traders, thieves and robbers—fall the sodomites and the effeminate. This is how the King James Version rendered *malakoi* and *arsenokoitai*, and it has guided our interpretation since.

To protect myself from Paul's vehemence—and the vitriol and self-conceit with which other Christians wield him—I learned to recite these words and their origins. *Malakoi* was a general ancient Greek term for male effeminateness: those who find hard labor intolerable, who overindulge in luxuries, who fight poorly in battle, who study too much. In first-century Greco-Roman culture, women were so inferior that any man who willingly took a woman's place—whether in being physically weak or choosing to be the "bottom" in a sexual encounter or wearing perfume to attract *female* partners—should be mocked. So too I did with *arsenokoitai*, with *porneia*, with *atimia*, taking the words apart and tracing their use throughout the Scriptures and ancient secular writings, trying to defend myself against those who happily took up the armor of God to beat me with the sword of the Spirit.[5]

This accomplished three things:

1. I was exhausted from carrying this information with me, ever-present in the back pocket of my mind for reference when someone felt the need to remind me those verses were there.

2. Those who had quoted Paul against me didn't care and, in fact, became more enraged and convinced of my apostasy when I tried to explain.

3. I hated Paul.

I hated him for how he had reinforced the standards of his day, for how he had failed to protect women and slaves, for how he had enshrined condemnation forever in holy writ. I wished I could sit him down and explain. I guessed he probably wouldn't have listened. He did not seem like the type to take advice well.

I mentioned my struggle to Deb, my supervising pastor, while I was serving as an intern in her church. Only in passing—I knew better than to openly admit to a fellow Christian that I hated Paul—but I murmured something about struggling with his persistent legalism.

She looked at me with compassion. "What did I ask you to do, when you started here?"

I blinked. "To—to get to know the people. To hear their stories, and to fall in love with them."

"Bingo," she replied.

I grumbled in response and opened the book of Acts. I began to retrace Paul's backstory. A young man, convicted in faith, watching the stoning of a seeming heretic. A righteous man on the warpath for the Lord. Well trained in scriptural interpretation and overly confident in his application.

Oh, no.

A perfectionist who pursued God with zeal but got knocked off his high horse and had to change everything he understood about faith? Explaining what God had done in his life, blending his experience with philosophy and Scriptures? Periodically horrified by what other so-called Christians were up to? Periodically his opinions on how everyone else should think and act were totally wrong?[6]

This was sounding irritatingly familiar.

When I was twenty-seven, I dragged myself down the street from my apartment to an Al-Anon meeting. The speaker, a woman my mother's age, introduced herself and began to tell her story. "I was divorced, I had two little kids, and I was twenty-seven—I thought my life was over!" She roared with laughter at the memory. The room laughed with her. I did not. I clung to the side of my chair and thought, *But my life really is over.*

Al-Anon is the partner organization to Alcoholics Anonymous. AA came first, with small groups around the nation gathering in church basements to talk about powerlessness and courage and transformation. After a short while, the partners and parents and children and friends of alcoholics—often gathered in the kitchens of those same church basements, so the story goes, brewing coffee and waiting for the meeting to end so they could drive those who had lost their licenses home—began to voice their own needs for a support group. And so Al-Anon, the organization for those who care about someone with a drinking problem, began. Using the same twelve steps that guided AA, the families and friends of alcoholics (in recovery or not) confessed their own powerlessness over alcohol, the unmanageability of their lives, the desperate need for courage and change. I went to Al-Anon first not because someone I loved was an active alcoholic but because I was desperate. A financial miscommunication at church had made me so tense that for two days I'd been unable to relax and slept so fitfully that I slammed my hand in the car door the next day. My church administrator, who was also dealing with the miscommunication, was far more level-headed. After it was all over, she mentioned that it was her Al-Anon experience that had helped her navigate the tension. Her voice was one in a line of many that suggested my uncontrollable panic—the fear in grocery stores, the struggle in class—might be helped by working the twelve steps.

I hated this suggestion. Yes, fine, my father had a complex relationship with alcohol, and had since I was a child. But I'd moved out five years ago, and I had no problems with drinking— okay, I had a few problems, but nothing that incapacitated me in any way. I wasn't living with or dating an active addict. I had such a low tolerance that two drinks was my limit. My all-consuming four-alarm-fire panic had nothing to do with alcohol. What was Al-Anon going to teach me? I went to Al-Anon almost out of spite, to prove I didn't belong, or at least that I could get all that I needed out of two meetings, maybe three, and then be done with it. In working the twelve steps—which, disappointingly, took much longer than three meetings to accomplish—I was introduced to my own god. It was not Jesus. It was not much of a higher power at all. It was other people.

I had spent most of the past five years dedicated to making sure everyone around me was content. My friends and my partner and my professors all thought I was capable and smart, attentive and generous with my time and energy. This, I thought, made me a good person and a good potential pastor. This, Al-Anon countered, might be what they called *codependency*.

Codependency has a variety of definitions and applications but essentially centers on emotional reliance on another person to the point that the self is subsumed. It happens often in relationships characterized by illness or addiction. Codependent people are well intentioned, trying to care for someone in pain, but their caretaking easily becomes enabling, allowing the sufferer to persist in their behavior (especially in cases of addiction). There is a "need to be needed," to protect the relationship at all costs. Codependent people name different fears as the source of their actions, but at the core, they are afraid of being abandoned and unlovable.

Some descriptions of codependency talk of becoming formless, molding ourselves to best fit others until we no longer know our own shape. In a desperate attempt to keep our loved ones close, we lose our own boundaries. Our emotions become porous, taking on whatever those around us feel, absorbing as much anger or sadness or pain as we can in the hope that we can create stasis. The dream was: if I could feel someone else's feelings for them, then they wouldn't feel them. If I could keep them happy by eliminating all their problems, they wouldn't leave me. And when the leaving happens—as it often does—we are completely unmoored. Having lost our shape to fit another, we no longer know who we are.

Sometimes I lost form by overcommitting. I gave myself away, stretched myself too thin, took on too much. This grew out of my perfectionism and project-love: I have always been fascinated by innovation grounded in reading, research, and reflection. Since I was a child I have thought that everything could be improved. This is not an unworthy idea, until I took it to what seemed like the next logical step: since I could see how things could be improved, why shouldn't I be the one to fix them? I was perpetually exhausted: what had I done that day? What had I failed to do? How could I have better allotted my time to meet the needs of everyone around me? I never would have described myself as trying to control others; I was just trying to help. I was the first to volunteer for everything. I craved leadership roles. I wanted to be the friend that everyone came to with their problems. I had to be bigger and better than who I actually was. If I could do everything, if I could be all things to all people, then I would never be weighed in the balance and found wanting.

In romantic relationships I could be incredibly charming, spending hours planning surprise dates or crafting personalized journals. I made sure the world knew I was joyously happy with whoever I was with. My love and happiness seemed expansive and complete. But within the relationship, I was making myself smaller and smaller. In each relationship, I compromised. I would voice a want gently, almost laughably, watching my girlfriend (whoever I was with at the time) for her reaction; the moment it was clear that she had not been clairvoyant enough to realize that my quick little joke was actually a devastating self-revelation of a deep need that was not being fulfilled, I slammed the lid tight on whatever I had asked for. I didn't really *need* commitment, compassion, compromise, marriage, sex. I had enough just by being with her. Didn't I? I would spend days in internal agony: should I end this? *No,* I always told myself. *Being with someone is better than being alone. Be thankful for what you have—it could be so much worse.*

Codependent people—often children, partners, or parents of addicts—know this self-segmentation. The relationship, not the health of the two people in it, is the priority. Confronting someone about how their choices jeopardize your needs risks the whole relationship. If I initiated confrontation, my girlfriend (or friend or family member) might leave, and then I would be in the worst of all possible situations: a failure, alone. Far better to compromise whatever I needed, to force myself to fit whatever the relationship could offer.

Of course, this never worked. The end took different forms on different timelines, but always there was an explosion: I could not fit the box I had forced myself into. I could not continue the compromise forever. I made this mistake, impressively, in quick succession, girlfriend after girlfriend: every time I began anew I promised myself that *this* time would be different, *this* time I would stand up for what I needed, *this* time I would be willing to walk away if I couldn't have it rather than begin again the cycle of pretending I'd never asked for it in the first place. Perhaps what was most tragic of all is my actions meant my relationships had no chance to be real; by being too afraid to ask for what I truly needed, I never gave my girlfriends the opportunity to meet those needs.

My Al-Anon journey, the unweaving of these tenacious hooks of codependency, took place at the same time as my ninety-day slog through the Bible. I was in the midst of the prophets when I finally acknowledged, scrawling it alongside the margins in my daily meditations from Hazelden, that God was not my God; other people were. I do not recommend this. The prophets have a lot to say about what the future of Israel when something other than God is at the center:

Therefore thus says the Holy One of Israel:
Because you reject this word, and put your trust in
    oppression and deceit,
and rely on them,
therefore this iniquity shall become for you
like a break in a high wall, about to collapse,
whose crash comes suddenly, in an instant.

Isaiah's words struck me in the chest. The walls were coming down around me. I had trusted in self-oppression, self-compromise, self-destruction; I had relied on deceit, on lies, on pretending to be far more capable than I was. Now everything was collapsing. Tears coursing down my face, I began to write my own translation:[7]

Thus says the Lord God, the Holy One of Israel:
Because you believed that appearance was more beautiful than vulnerability,
    and put your trust in control rather than truth,
an honest word will shatter you, and revelation will be like a crack in a high dam.
If you will not cede control, it will be wrested from you.
If you sacrifice your soul to protect a facade,
    then God will free you by shattering it beyond repair.
There will be no shield to give yourself cover, not a sliver left to hide behind.
The only safety left for you will be in the shelter of God's wings.
Only in surrender will you find the power you have longed for;
    only when you let go will you be strong.
If you try to run, the truth will follow you.
If you hide, you will find honesty still with you.
The cave where you conceal your heart will be filled with light that searches you out.
But do not be afraid.

With each step, solid ground will rise to meet you,
and you will hear a voice behind your shoulder, saying,
"Yes. This is what you were made for."

I began to understand what idolatry was like. The prophets' cries for justice had long been my signposts for freedom; now I turned also to their cries for a life centered on God. I thought of Paul, the would-be Pharisee, constraining himself to his legalistic interpretation of the law. I thought of the violence he dealt onto others. He needed to control the religious conversation so much that he would rather imprison and silence the "Followers of the Way" than allow for something new to happen within his faith. I saw in him my own judge, jury, and executioner; I saw all the times that I'd locked up my possibilities for change, silenced my own cries for liberation and salvation. I had refused, time and time again, to face the fact that how I lived my life, with others at the center of it all, was crushing me and trapping them. Now I was faced with the story of a fellow perfectionist, so sure that he had been right when he was so very wrong, standing at the altar of an unknown god and saying: *I too have misunderstood who God was. Let me tell you now what I know.*[8]

I followed Paul to Macedonia and Greece, into the city of Troas, into the upper room where he preached from dusk till dawn. I knew what this was like, to be so excited about what God had done, to be wide-awake with dancing hands as I told the stories of how far I had come from where I'd once been. With Paul I set my face toward Jerusalem, toward the religious elite who would try to silence me and claim I had flouted laws and desecrated holy ground. I was coming to know him not as my opposition but as my brother, as flawed as I was but as hopeful too.[9]

I heard his hope in the letters he wrote to his communities. He planted churches and then moved on, trusting in the work of the Spirit to move them more toward Christ, only to receive letters with questions that could not be answered. Scholars consider his letter to the church in Thessalonika the first written words of the New Testament (predating the Gospels). Our best guess, considering the content of his letter, is that his new church was confused: he had promised the return of Jesus, to gather the faithful and transform the world, but instead Jesus had not yet returned, and faithful members of the community had died. Death was supposed to be conquered; Christ was supposed to be victorious. How could this have happened? I imagined Paul pacing his tent, dictating to his scribe: *Do not grieve as those do who have no hope. Death is not the end of the story; those who have gone on before us will not be away from us for long.*[10] I comforted in Paul's promise of Jesus, both powerful enough to resurrect the dead and humble enough to take on flesh.

I saw Paul's love, both for Christ and for the communities he planted, and opened up to wonder if that love was wide enough for me, too. In his expansive offering of the Lord's Supper, I saw the same wideness that had been offered to me.[11] There was to be no holding back, no preferential treatment, no better or worse person to receive and to share: we are to share in the one bread, one cup, without distinction based on wealth or race or origin—or, I wondered, perhaps even without distinction based on gender and sexuality. Perhaps the charisma of the Spirit could too be found in me, in my gender and my sexuality: gifts of discernment, gifts of wisdom, gifts of hope wrought from pain and compassion wrought from rejection. Maybe I too was part of the body of Christ, along with the whole queer and trans family. Perhaps that love that abides, the love that overcomes all, the love that is without fear, the love that is greatest of all, was love for me too.

I heard Paul's anger and comforted in it. When the church in Galatia was stricken with the disease of legalism, when "Christians" had followed in Paul's footsteps to add that the good news of Christ was all well and good, but circumcision was required, I heard the story of my own faith. I saw Jess's eyes flash with the same passion the circumcision faction must have preached: "What sin has been put on your heart that you thought you could obtain the grace of God so easily?" I saw in the Galatians the brokenheartedness of my queer family, so close to Christ and now dragged violently away. I began to read Paul's words as if he had spoken them to the churches that would cast me out: *Are you so quickly deserting the gospel? Did you receive the Spirit through the works of the law, or by believing what you heard? For the whole law is summed up in a single commandment: You shall love your neighbor as yourself.*[12]

I heard in all this a promise, greater than Paul's social location, stronger than his failure to know how long the church would rest on and abuse his commands to local congregations. If I could forgive myself for all the idolatry I had practiced, if I could believe that God could forgive and restore me, perhaps too my brother Paul could be released. Surely my own emails will not stand up to scrutiny in twenty years, much less in two thousand. I could treat my brother separately than the church who, in bondage to its own love of power and control, had happily taken up his words to wound those who needed the most protection.

Perhaps Paul, at the great feast in heaven, will be seated next to all those who have known his words best as bruise rather than gift. Perhaps we will be up from dinner till dawn, nowhere to go, no urgency to our words, no Jerusalem to set our face to, no rules to fear and no powers to placate. We will tell him our stories—how the scrappy little sect of Judaism called "The Way" became bound to the empire of Rome, how cities and cultures across creation were crushed into homogeny and forced into a faith he wanted to be free, how his words became walls and weapons. I imagine our hands in his as we tell of the unexpected joys—how we out on the edges found each other, how the body divided could not remain so, how each community that had been a conduit for the gospel in our own lives had broken free of legalism and grabbed hold of the grace that had never let go of us. I imagine an addendum, in Paul's bold strokes:[13]

> Neither death nor life, nor angels nor rulers, not things present or things to come,
> nor laws, nor legalism or infallibility,
> nor powers of misogyny or white supremacy or queerphobia or transphobia,

nor height of self-righteousness nor depth of condemnation and despair,
nor anything else in all creation
will be able to separate us from the love of God in Christ Jesus our Lord.

CHAPTER 9

I miss my father.

Not the man that died two months shy of his eighty-eighth birthday, a few weeks past my parents' thirty-third wedding anniversary. Not the man whose slow physical decline compromised in turns his body, his mind, and his heart. Not the man whose prescriptions increased while his world decreased. I do not miss that man—not because I did not love him, but because his world was so small that I cannot wish him back in it.

I miss the man that made me. He was fifty-seven when I was born, twenty-three years older than my mother. The day after my birth, he passed out candy cigars on the floor of the Minnesota legislature, networking with the state politicians, raising more funds for the university where he served as vice president. He was gregarious, charming, with a brilliant mind and a quick wit. He was charismatic and self-confident, unafraid of his choices, so much so that once when he was challenged by a departmental opponent he sent back a single typewritten line on university letterhead: *Pardon me, sir, you obviously mistake me for someone who gives a shit.* He admired strong teachers and researchers, regardless of race, religion, or sexual orientation. He advocated for an out lesbian at a time when her sexuality could have cost her her job. The stress of his work made him unpredictable. But when he was happy, his love was enormous, as tall and broad as him, as strong as the arms that had built the decks around our house.

His life was bookended by scarcity. A child of the Depression, he learned to scrimp and save, to work harder and smarter than those around him, to take opportunities when they arose and press on when they were absent. The GI Bill turned him from a farm boy to a sharpshooter to an English professor. He raised five children, four of them with his first wife, who died in the mid-seventies before mental illness or trauma or grief was any kind of national conversation. Raised Catholic, he settled with my mother and me in the Episcopal Church but kept a rosary by his chair and murmured the Our Father in the German he'd grown up with.

He taught me how to write a proper essay with a powerful conclusion, how to read voraciously and compare books about the same event to dig up the reality behind the separate truths. But as my world grew, his shrank. He retired earlier than he wanted to, his body unable to recover fully after a sudden ruptured appendix took him to the emergency room the day before my sixth birthday. His eyesight went, then his hip, then his heart, then his knees, then his lungs. Over the next twenty years he faced multiple illnesses and several major surgeries. His sharp mind dulled. His memory was sometimes crisp, other times faded and fractured. His sickness took him far into the dark. He hated having his credit cards taken from him after losing them. He grumbled when we reduced the sugar in the house to control his diabetes. He was furious the first time I refused to go to the store for another magnum of cheap cabernet, ignoring my concerns that his opiate use was becoming complicated by the alcohol.

And I wonder who he will be, when we meet again at the great feast in the kingdom.

When we have passed through the refining fire, when everything that cannot come into the kingdom of God has been seared from us like impurities in dark-shining gold, who will we be?[1] Who are politicians and pastors without their power? Who are abusers and addicts without control? What will Christianity be without anti-Semitism and Islamophobia, without racism and misogyny? Who will my father be, without the pain that marked him all my adult life?

Who will I be? If my codependency and anxiety are burned away—easy as thin bark at the edge of a log—I might, then, come to know what it is to love without fear. If the fog of my depression is finally and forever scattered by the flames of the Spirit, I might feel the depths of emotion that have been dulled for me, might be able to weep without the terror that I will not come back from letting myself cry. If I could let go of the racism my culture and nation and church has given me to cover my eyes and ears from the truth of our history and present—I might, then, witness without reserve the iridescent beauty of the children of God. If my wounds from the hands of a Bible-banging church turn in one eternal moment from scar to cauterized skin to brand-new flesh—I might, then, know what it is like to stand among the family of God and feel no need for self-protection, no desire to build an armor of apologetics.

Who will my beloveds be? My friends and queer family marred by the hate of those who have beaten them with the word and driven them from the church—what will they look like? I remember that Jesus, the first fruits of those raised from the dead, was not without his scars. They were part of the risen body. They had made him who he was and proved that he was more than anyone had bargained for. The body of God had been and would always now be marked by the murderous hearts of men who craved power and control. What has been done to us, the lessons and the proof in it, does not fade. The resurrection does not make us unhurt. It makes us whole.

Toward the end of his life, my father placed a card near the window where he sat every morning for breakfast. It was a quote from Dorothy Day, social activist and servant of God:

> I really only love God as much as I love the person I love the least.

Dorothy knew, and my father was learning, and I learned from him, that love is neither the beginning of the kingdom, nor the end. It is the kingdom itself. It is all-encompassing. It is the whole process, from start to finish. And as my father's life waned, he set his face toward the kingdom, knowing it was time—in his imperfect, carbon-bound, fully human way—to shed whatever held him back from that practice of love. He knew he couldn't take anything else with him. He knew everything else would be ash.

I did not like the quote then, and I don't much care for it now. There are plenty of people that I think I have very good reason to love only a little. Another church issues a statement denouncing the "idle tales" of the dozens of "attention-hungry" victims who have come forward with accusations of long-standing sexual abuse by the pastor or priest. Another railroaded political process strips away voting opportunities for people of color or health insurance for the chronically ill or benefits for working women and their children. Another stranger messages me to ask how I reconcile my faith and my sexuality, which turns out not to be a philosophical exercise but a life-and-death question for a teenager who can't keep pretending not to be queer but also won't survive on the street her parents have threatened her with. I am quite content on those days to load up my spiritual rifle with Bible bullet after Bible bullet about oppression and hypocrisy and proper care of the neighbor. The sword of the Spirit weighs heavy in my hands; once it split me in two, but now I am ready to turn it on the hearts of those who have opposed me. I am ready to celebrate others' forced march into the flames, where the rich and the judgmental will burn in unquenchable fire. I feel justified in my anger.

And I feel justified because I know the sharp edges of the word *love*. "Love" has been wielded by Christians who cloak their unkindness as "hate the sin, love the sinner," who claim to "speak the truth in love" no matter what damage it does. But when one person says it's love and the other person walks away wounded, we don't call that love or truth or grace. We call it abuse.

I know, too, how "love" has covered all manner of sins. I know churches that profess to love and consider that an acceptable substitute for affirmation or celebration. I know people who act as if the feeling of love acquits them from its work, as if love did not mean active participation in freeing those oppressed from the system that ground them down. And every time those who called me sister fail to look out for me like family, I am reminded too of my own failings. There are plenty of times I failed to notice the marginalization and passive silencing of others. How many churches have I served that were all white? How often have I unquestioningly moved in female-only spaces without asking if my trans sisters were welcome alongside me? I do not always see the steps where there were no chair lifts, the unamplified sound, the intense stimuli that prevented many from full participation in the body of Christ. I know how easy it is to pretend that love frees me from such trivialities.

I know, too, that love does not heal all wounds. It may bear and endure all things, but it does not heal them. Many of my queer and trans family, finding simple and forthright acceptance in a friend or a pastor or a congregation, feel the freedom of the love that heals. What they have needed is to know they are loved and accepted, just as they are. Many others of us find no freedom in acceptance. Those who have suffered trauma, who are wounded by the world or by God's church, who are broken in spirit in ways that do not bounce back, are not mystically unburdened in one shining moment. We remain agitated and hypervigilant. Worship or Bible study floods us with hostility, anxiety, or suspicion. We self-destruct or socially isolate. We have had our faith stripped from us or had to let it go when it beat us. We are sifting through the ashes of what once seemed unshakeable. After what is often years of spiritual abuse, we are not easily mended.

Any pastor or congregation who welcomes back those who have been so wounded—no matter what the abuse took root in—takes a great risk. We are not easy to minister to. We question everything. We flinch at sermons on *sin* and *holiness* and *the righteous*. Bible quotes on phone backgrounds make us uneasy. Songs and stories of Scripture that rely heavily on a father God of condemning judgment send us for the door. Inclusion, much as it is necessary for healing, does not negate the spiritual trauma we bear. The work of liberating love, love that casts out our fear and binds up our broken hearts, love that penetrates so deeply it allows us to believe the impossibility that we might actually *be* lovable, is a process without an obvious end.

I know the mercy of God both too well and not enough to think I am wise enough to measure it out. I know the danger in damning others, much as on my troubled days I relish it. I know the temptation to become what I have rejected. I have seen what the power of "God's word" does in the hands of the religious elite (among whom I am numbered). I believe that turning the world upside down does not mean restructuring all the painful oppressive systems with the survivors on top and the oppressors crushed.

I do not like this. I am still too wounded, this side of the veil, and too protective. At my best, I can confess to hoping that I might someday believe in a table wide enough for all of us.

Many of the faithful come to God fragmented, broken by the world's pressures—or worse, by blows from a church that has maligned or condemned us. We still dare to come back to faith, despite the danger. And God witnesses us. God sees our wounds and recognizes the pain that God-in-flesh knew: hatred and vitriol, rejection and condemnation, beating and crucifixion. When no one else does, God sees—and God weeps. God does not rejoice in our suffering. God hates that we hurt. God hears the cries of the slave, of those crushed under others' hunger for power and control. God hears the pleas of the orphan and widow, the marginalized and forgotten in societies that rely on productivity as a measure of wealth. Through the prophet Jeremiah, God condemned the priests whose greed and injustice closed their eyes to the suffering of the people.

That is who God is—the God who hears, and then the God who acts. God does not remain removed, nor is God immovable. God acts. God is troubled by our cries and moves to alleviate them. God inspired the midwives of the Hebrew slaves who would not kill the baby boys so longed for. God called to Moses and spoke through his stumbling mouth to command Pharaoh: *Let my people go.* God saw how the people of Israel began to reproduce the violence of Egypt, hoarding food and demanding control. *Is that what you think I freed you for?* God murmured. *Try again.* And there were rules and lessons, forty years of them, and it didn't take long before crossing the Jordan and laying waste to the cities of Canaan that the people of God began to forget again. Power—political, religious, financial, personal—is addictive. And so God sent prophets and preachers, advocates for the poor and the oppressed, who challenged gods that bled the people dry with the promise of control and spoke instead of the God who upended all our attempts at it.[2]

And then God put on flesh.

The religious elites saw nothing but an itinerant and untrained teacher upsetting the status quo. The political powers wanted nothing to do with it, as long as it stayed out of their business of taxation and conquest. In the rampant suffering around him, in the faces of the demon-possessed and leprous and crippled and dying, Jesus did not turn away and murmur, "This is your cross to bear." He did not examine their doctrine and assess how closely they aligned to the theologies of the dominant culture. All we know is they believed he could cure them—and he did.

God was willing to be subject to the whims of the world. Knowing just how violently power protects itself, how happily the oppressed will turn complicit if it means murder is dealt elsewhere that day—God showed up anyway and stood on the side of everyone the world called worthless. God sat on the side of a grassy mountain and said: *Nothing is as it seems. You think the rich and joyful are the blessed; it is the poor and the grieving who will receive far more than they need. You think it is the powerful and the full who own the earth; it is the hungry and meek who will inherit it all. You think it is the ones who are praised and uplifted, the rightfully proud, the elite, and the righteous who are blessed; it is you, you who will inherit my message of mercy, you who will be mocked for how I overturn the world.*[3]

There is a long-standing practice in Christianity of commanding a victim to "turn the other cheek." Jesus demanded it, religious leaders remind us: *Do not resist an evildoer. If anyone strikes you on the right cheek, turn the other also.*[4] Submit to your abuser; take what is coming for you; receive the blows as Christ received the whips and spits and mockery of his crucifiers. Pacifism and nonviolence is the way to true discipleship. It doesn't take much historical or contemporary examination to notice that the church itself has been a bit hit and miss with the application of this teaching. For women who were abused? Absolutely. For black people under the pressured fire hoses of police? Check. But when it comes to nuclear disarmament or the development of unmanned drones, we are somehow completely fine striking back. We don't just resist the evildoers, we annihilate them. Turning the other cheek is a poor political policy. We're only interested in it when it requires no sacrifice on our part, when Jesus's mandate conveniently reinforces the status quo. "Turn the other cheek" implies "and shut your mouth about it."

The fascinating cultural story of Jesus's time, when I sat on the text long enough, went deeper than that. The striker would have been right-handed—as with 85 percent of the population today, and possibly more simply from cultural expectations. For a right-handed person to strike someone else on the right cheek, they had to backhand them. And backhanding, in that time, was an action that a superior took on an inferior: a husband on a wife, a parent on a child, a master on a slave. It was more than a blow; it was a reminder: *you are beneath me.*

But to strike the left cheek with the right hand required an open palm or a fist—a slap or a punch. And those were ways of fighting between *equals.* So to *turn the other cheek* was to defiantly look the husband, the father, the master in the eye and say: *Go ahead and hit me again, but don't forget that we are equals in the eyes of God. You are not above me. You may have the strength to hit me, but I will retain the right to hit you back— and when I do not take it, I will make it clear before heaven and earth who is the true superior in this moment. I will not let your violence make me forget who I am and whose I am.*

I began to imagine that fearsome strength in the eyes of women who would not take another blow, who finally picked up the phone and called a friend and said *Come get me. I am worth more than this.* I began to see it in the eyes of children and teens and young adults who refused to take their abusive parents' condemnation. I see it now in the fierce and dark-shining power of the Black Lives Matter movement, who stand in streets and highways, who kneel on football fields, who will not bow their heads but who raise their voices to say *Enough. Enough. Enough.* I see it now in the eyes of every queer and trans person who refused to stay in churches that beat them with Scripture over and over again yet dare to keep coming back to God.

I saw it in the faces of those who taught me to say "No." We gathered in upper rooms in metal folding chairs with decaf coffee mostly just to have something warm to hold in our hands. My teachers were not experts. They were not trained. Their only power was that they knew their own story. And so each week together we'd confess: *We admitted we were powerless over alcohol, that our lives had become unmanageable.* Each week they talked about the power of "no"—the strength of knowing that there was a higher purpose for us than to mold ourselves to the people around us. They taught me how to claim my own light. They told me, "Don't set yourself on fire to keep someone else warm."

In their faces, I saw the women waiting for the bridegroom. There were five foolish and five wise, and the foolish said, *Give us some of your oil, for our lamps are going out.*[5] For years I had wrestled with and been unblessed by this parable, a story that seemed to approve of selfishness and condemn the unprepared. But in the faces of those wise bridesmaids now I saw the exhaustion of women who had finally learned to care for themselves. They knew that giving themselves away, sharing the oil they had so carefully curated, would leave everyone without light. They had stopped apologizing for not being all things to all people. They had finally learned to say, "I've done my work. Now you must do yours." To be allowed to boundary ourselves, to say "No," was one of the crucial steps in believing the impossibility of our own belovedness.

Al-Anon, like Scripture, was a series of miracles tucked into stories. Sin and shame and brokenness are isolating, making us think that we are alone. In a place made safe for our stories, for the tenderest parts of ourselves, I have seen how love is all about communing. Love brings us together, and it also requires us together; love on our own is an exercise in going in circles. But love in a community, love where we hear each other's stories, where we witness to each other's brokenness and share in a hope for transformation—that, beloveds, is where I have seen the kingdom of heaven.

In the sharing of stories, I have seen the lies of the enemy slowly burned away. The rejection of the world's proclamations that we are broken and wretched, that our trauma is our burden to carry, that oppression is just the way it's always been and the way it will always be. Instead, I have heard the proclamation of promise that God's mercy and compassion have enveloped us, have given us boundaries, have pierced our hearts to open us up to love.

But all this, of course, takes time—an allowance not often offered to victims and survivors. The church has happily rushed to a demand for forgiveness before a perpetrator has even opened his mouth to claim his sin. *Jesus said to forgive seventy times seven*, the powers-that-be whisper through a scowl. *That would have essentially been an infinite amount, by the counting standards of his time.* They ignore, conveniently, the preceding verses where Jesus outlines the process for restoration: when a sin is committed, first tell the sinner to his face, and if he will not listen then tell two more and try again with witnesses, and if he will not listen tell it to the *whole church*. Such a rebuke would have been a conversation between equals; once the power dynamic of abuse enters the conversation, Jesus's words ring ever clearer: *It is not the will of your Father in heaven that one of these little ones should be lost.*[6] What if every church suddenly facing the racism or queerphobia or sexual assault within their walls cleared the altar and opened the pulpit for every victim and survivor to stand up and say: *Here is what was done to me.*

Not only must the perpetrator and the whole church listen, but for there to be forgiveness there must be repentance. Repentance is not "I'm sorry," and it is not "I'm sorry and I'll try to make sure no one catches me at it again," and it is absolutely not "I'm sorry that you were hurt by God's truth." Repentance, in the original Greek, is based on a physical action, *metanoia*: turning around. Repentance means seeing how far we have gone off the path and making a hasty U-turn and a sprint back. "Repent and believe in the good news!" cannot be translated into "Say you're sorry but make no changes and offer no reparations!" And yet this is the kind of forgiveness we suggest for survivors, to accept the "I'm *sorry*" of a smirking sibling forced to comply and fully intent on doing it again. No. Forgiveness takes repentance, repentance takes change, and healing takes time. Without these, the wounds only fester. My queer family knows what it is like to be shut out of heaven, and my wounds combined with my ego have happily populated hell with those who have condemned us. There has been little grace in this. The tighter I have built walls around the table, the quicker I have found Jesus on the other side of them, working always again for the offensiveness of grace, the ridiculous possibility of repentance and reparation. I will admit I do not have the patience of Christ. I want to know exactly how long all this is going to take.

In my first semester of college, I took astronomy for a science credit. The math and physics fascinated me, but not nearly as much as our professor's sudden tangent in mid-December: "This won't be on the final," he said, and proceeded to explain that space and time are linked. They don't operate independently. Time is, in fact, the fourth dimension. The singular "space-time" can be used to signify where a particular event occurs. This aligns with any basic concept of history, which understands that events in time do not occur without a location. But it *also* means that, if the universe is continuously expanding (and he explained how it is, based on cosmological redshift), and the universe was once *not* expanding and was an infinitely dense singular point of mass until the metric expansion of space began suddenly and without explanation, then just as space began with the Big Bang, so did *time*.

Oh, *wow*, I thought, although I could not explain why this felt so significant. It would not be until six years later that the other piece of the puzzle fell into place, in my eschatology class. In *that* course, my professor presented us with a view of heaven that attested to God's existence not only outside of space but also outside of time. "If space and time are linked," he said, so matter-of-factly that I nearly fell out of my chair, "and we think God is outside space, should not God also be outside of time? And thus, would we not, too, be outside of time when we are with God?"

Physics, it appears, would be my resolution between this life and the next. How long would we suffer in the flames that purified us from all that was not Love? Who would be at the gates waiting for me and how long had they had to wait and what age would they be? Once inside, how would I not be bored by thousands upon thousands of years of praise worship? The answer was: space and time are one, and God is outside all of them. There is no "how long," no "waiting," no "thousands of years." I am already there, for there is no already and no there. The moment of healing and reconciliation would be upon me before I could know it, because there was no moment and no eternity.

In a world so divided, I am not sure we are ready to believe that the table of heaven can be so impossibly wide. Yet I cannot find, either in my experience of faith or in the stories of Scripture, any promise that does not lead to offensively miraculous reconciliation. All my scars, like Jesus's, would still be there. They would be proof of who I was and what I had survived. And yet I will be seated next to those who had dealt them upon me, in a time and place that was neither, in a space I could not imagine where I could feel entirely protected. I will feel boundaried and bound-up, not only able to say "no" but never asked a question to which my answer would not be "yes." I will know forgiveness face-to-face, like a brother beside me at the table and not a power from on high. I will have the time and space to heal without space-time in which to be wounded. I will hear my family's stories, all of them, overlapping and instantaneous, for there will be no "me first" and "but what if," only an expanse of time in which there is no hurry to finish, no work to get back to, no running out of good wine.

Most of us, I think, will experience only the smallest sample of such unbounded timelessness on this side of the veil. We struggle for resolution, building steps one at a time toward sanctification, but I am required to confess to my own reality: even at my very best, at my most joyfully serene or defiantly courageous, I am still far short of the glory of God. Perhaps I am bound by the stain of original sin; perhaps carbon-made and conscious creatures are too bound by fear of death to release themselves completely. There are a hundred explanations in between for how we have come to be who we are, wounded by others and by ourselves, desperately wanting in our best moments to shower the world in abundant love and yet never quite there. But even though we cannot achieve perfection on this earth, I long for us to try. Not to satisfy the long-standing point system of organized religion—in which right action and right belief earn us an eternity of glory and spare us the eternity of supposedly deserved punishment—but because if we will find ourselves seated at the same long spread in heaven, it might be best if I stop kicking you under the table now. If we are bound up together, if the trajectory of the kingdom is toward our re-collection as the children of God, then to persist in unkindness and injustice toward ourselves and our fellow humans on earth is to actively deny our future. If one day we will eat with God, then each day on earth we are invited to learn how.

There will be more than enough to spare, like a desert camp was covered with a fine, flaky frost, thin and crisp and honey-sweet, family, never any left over. This is what it means to eat with God, the story says: *greed and fear will rot, for there is enough for everyone.* This is what it means to eat with God, the story says: *and all ate and were filled, and there were twelve baskets left over.* This is what it means to eat with God, the story says: *let everyone who is thirsty, come.*[7]

And I will see my father again.

CHAPTER 10

found

All of us have special ones who have loved us into being.

—Rev. Fred McFeely Rogers, aka Mister Rogers

I have come to love the stories of Scripture because I was found by love first. From my first days I was wrapped in a mother's fierce and protective love; it was an easy transition to believe that God, too, loved me like a thick knit blanket, close and comforting, keeping me safe. I have come to trust the stories that best lift up that love: the mighty force that took the people out of slavery and, over forty years, then took the slavery out of the people; the prophets who demanded satisfaction for the weak and oppressed; the cry of Mary, her child who was the child of the whole world turning in her womb, as she sang the song of her ancestor Hannah: *My soul magnifies the Lord, and my spirit rejoices in God my savior, for you have looked with favor on your humble servant.*[1]

I am found by a divine love that is invitational. It is not forceful or demanding, insisting on its own way, irritable and resentful. Love is a dance to which God extends a hand. I know what better theologians have surmised about the capacity of my own free will, but my experience and the stories of Scripture have borne the reality that I felt I had a choice. I could have walked away. I still could. But there is something in the story that compels me, something in the promise of love that dares me to try despite the dangers I have met before. I am not yet ready to give up on the church, or on Scripture, or on God. The invitation has been made open to me, and each day that I have taken it, I have found myself in the midst of a celebration, surrounded by the resounding cry: *Rejoice with me, for I have found my coin.*[2]

I am found by a divine love that is merciful. This love is patient and kind; love knows me, far better than I know myself, and loves me still. This love has the capacity to keep a record of my sins, even longer than my perfectionist brain could begin to surmise, and yet is unconcerned. I know the dangers of what nonplussed love can do, as if it invalidates all consequences and frees me to my own wiles. But the mercy that finds me is not cheap; it is free, and it costs everything. This grace knows how fully bare I had already made myself to my own faults. This mercy sees how much I am broken already. This mercy binds me up again.

This merciful love goes beyond forgiveness; it puts the salve in salvation, easing the weariness with which I have carried my own failures. I do not need a God who burdens me; I carry more than enough guilt on my own. What I found in mercy instead was a love that offers an easy yoke and a lighter load.[3] I am found by a love consistent even in my inconsistencies, persistently present despite the lies of the world or the missteps of my own feet. Love does not leave me. Love is new every morning, like a faithful dog laid across the bottom of my bed, ready again for a fresh day and a clean start. Love does not leave when I fail, nor can the world or the church hide it from me for long.

I am found by a divine love that heals. There is no condemnation in it. Love is not afraid of my sin or my brokenness. The darkness of my depression is not dark to this love; night is as bright as day. There is no soft chuckle of self-satisfaction as my burden is pushed back onto me, no shrug of the divine shoulders or patronizing pat on my elbow with the words "It's just your cross to bear." Love stands beside my bed and says, *Little girl, get up.* When the crowd pushes me back, when my shame is too great to speak and all I can do is stretch out one shaking hand, love looks down to me and says, *Your faith has made you well.*[4] I cannot confess to much faith in these moments—more like desperation, a willingness to admit that I am not God and maybe something else might be. No matter how much I cling to my codependency and perfectionism, love looks at them and says, *Get out.* No matter how often I welcome them back, love lifts them again the moment I ask.

I am found by a divine love that comes close. Love does not sit far-off, cross-legged, uninterested in my days except to tally my wrongs. Love had once appeared in blazing bushes and flickers of flame in the darkness, in sheer silence on the mountaintop and in a voice that split the skies at love's own baptism. Love came close and walked beside me. Love broke bread, and love was the bread, tenderly offered to me, a promise of eternal presence.[5]

I am found by a divine love that is expansive. Every time I have reached the edge of how far I believed love could go, I have found myself instead standing in the middle of where love has already been. Love is not up for in-groups and out-groups, for tents that can only stretch so far or tables that can only seat so many. Love keeps going. Love casts a wider net each time and drops itself down from the heavens burdened with uncleanliness to cry out, *What I have called clean you must not call unclean.* Love has no tolerance for intolerance. When the people of God told stories of exclusion, the men casting out their foreign wives and children, love wrote the story of Ruth, the foreigner as or more loyal than any woman of Israel.[6]

I am found by a divine love that is unconditional and yet has expectations. Love does not keep space for cruelty or violence. Love laid down laws about leaving enough for the poor to glean and sacrificing only what a family could afford.[7] With every lie the world told about the glory of power and the power of glory, love blows against it, an unstoppable force against an object that claims immovability and yet could not stand against the whisper of God.

I am not found by this love all at once. There is no step-by-step process to getting found; in grief counseling, we know now that the "process of grief" is not a linear path by which we move from one stage to another but a single point that passes through five dimensions of reaction, looping and cycling, often in multiple directions at once. The same has been true for getting found. Each day brings a new aspect that I had not yet anticipated. Each experience moves me along to a new point within a dimension that I thought I'd already exhausted. My perfectionism has had to tangle with the reality that, on this side of the veil, I will accomplish none of this completely. I am now and not yet found. I cannot reach the end of it. All I can do is witness to what delivered me here, what is reaching out for all of us.

I am coming to believe that I am beloved. This happens, at best, for about eight minutes a week. Most of the time I am more convinced of my own depravity than the best Calvinist. Yet I am learning to reject what the world has offered; I am learning to believe that I am made in the image of God, fearfully and wonderfully. I have had no trouble believing that God loves everyone else (well, most of you), but it has been a long walk to accept that God might love me. Yet that is the reality that finds me in the stories of Scripture and in the proclamation of the gospel.

I have not only come to believe this spiritually; I am coming to know it in relationship and community. I was loved fiercely into being by my mother. I have known what it is to be surrounded by friends who know me and love me without compromise. My friends have called me back to myself when I have ventured too far down the road of what I thought I should be; they have pushed me beyond my own insecurities to claim my right as a child of God. And in my wife, Michelle, I have come to know the raw terror of being loved and trusted for who I am—not valued for what I can do or rejected for what I have done, but treasured and celebrated simply and consistently for who I am at the end of the day, when all the work and play is done and there is only my tired body and my open heart. What I am most afraid of, what makes me shy or anxious or self-loathing, she holds with tender care and such compassion that it is every day less possible for me to fear it.

There are days I doubt my belovedness. These are the days when anxiety wracks me, when my workaholic productivity drains me, when the snarls of those who would deny my call are louder than the whispers of God. These are the days I opt to lie to myself. *You are not worthless*, I murmur, even as my brain kicks back with a list of all I've failed to do. *You are not despised*, I promise, even when my heart cracks. *You are not alone*, I hum, even when my hands and feet ache with a solitary day's work. I call my friends. I wash the dishes. I take a scalding hot bath until my body and mind and soul realign and I am able to believe the lies—which were real, all along, even when I could not receive them. On the best of my worst days, I can act as if I am beloved, until I believe it again.

This love is not only for me. This expansive impossibility of inherent worth is etched on the heart of every one of us. We long for it, for acceptance and welcome and celebration. Our hearts hunger for the open recognition that we are more than our mistakes, that we have the capacity to grow beyond the practices that hold us back, that we are part of something greater than our own wants and needs. In the Scriptures, by the God of the Scriptures, we are reminded of the truth that has long wanted to resound within us: we are wonderfully made and endlessly treasured, both by the God who first made us and by the community of those who see us, in this life or the next, as we truly are.

I am claiming my own story. My story does not begin with me. I am woven into a long line of stories, the lives of my ancestors, not only those who gave birth to those who gave birth to me, but all those who have walked before me in faith. I claim the stories of Scripture as my stories, too. I find myself in the stories of the least, neglected or abused by the stronger but not forgotten by God; in the stories of impossibility, of water in the desert and food in time of drought; in the stories of the women who would not accept their cultural roles but pushed through to sit at the feet of Jesus.

I claim the stories of history that have made me who I am. I carry the stories of immigrant waves of Europe to America, of backbreaking work in factories and quarries. I carry the stories of women who refused to resign themselves to their place, who aspired to education and leadership, who saw the holes in the world and called themselves strong enough to mend them.

I carry the stories of my queer family, following in the footfalls of the trans black women who led us at Stonewall and the lesbians who cared for their gay brothers dying of AIDS and the histories upon histories of those who have never quite fit into what the world wanted them to be. I claim my family's story, my father's charm and my mother's prayers.

I claim, too, my own story: the joys of childhood, the loneliness of adolescence, the aching teenage years when I dwelled in how far from everyone else I would always be. I claim my successes, my persistence, my stubbornness. I claim the claim that God has on me.

I am learning to claim the faults of all of it, too. I refuse to be numb to the words of Scripture that wound my family of faith. I refuse to pretend that the holy writ of my religion and profession has not been a weapon in the hands of the hateful. There are words in it that are not of God. There is rape, genocide, abundant hatred stamped "Approved by God" by the victors who wrote the books. I cannot pretend this is not true. I can only confess I do not believe that stamp is real.

I am claiming the faults of my history. My parents' home, before it was a suburb, before the suburbs rose from cow farmland, was inhabited by the Dakota tribes. My father went to college on the GI Bill, a luxury afforded to white enlistees but not to men of color. My mother's immigrant family was able to succeed; by the time of my mother's birth, we were no longer coded as "nonwhite," and by the time of my birth, the question of my ethnicity mattered only to explain my dark brown hair in a sea of Minnesota blonde. My classroom difficulties were excused more easily than those of my peers of color. I serve a congregation of the Evangelical Lutheran Church in America, the least racially diverse and most white denomination in America. I cannot change all the facts of my past, but that does not mean I fail to be responsible for the present and the future.

I claim my sins. I have failed many times. I have hurt those I claimed to love, sometimes deeply. I am learning to face my faults, to stare back into the terror of what I have done, and not to cower and weep and beg for release but to accept that I have fallen short—even while I am still beloved. I have mended what I could and worked to release what I could not. I claim the sins of others against me and tell the story of how I could be knocked aside but never stay down. I claim, too, that which in me is broken and turned against myself: my depression, my anxiety, my codependency, my perfectionism. I have tried to be unafraid. I am not always successful.

To claim the truth and wholeness of a life's story is not only for me. The practice of confession and repentance laid the foundation for Christian life from the beginning. Despite the many ways in which the powers that be have corrupted it for their own gain, it remains an integral part of our life centered in the God of the Scriptures. God is not afraid of the truth about us. God is not shocked by it. God likely already knows it. We join in with that divine fearlessness when we face our own mistakes, things done and left undone, our individual actions and the systems in which we are complicit. We are the sum of who we have been and who we are and who we might yet become, and to own that truth is to bear witness to a God who can make miracles out of mess.

I am called to act in love for others. The love of God is not reserved only for me. Love is meant to knit us into community, into belief practiced in active love for our neighbor (who is, inconveniently, best described by Jesus as *anyone in need*).

Love calls me to be honest. I cannot turn my face away from my fellow children of God whom I have hurt, intentionally or not, by things done or left undone. Love calls me to own up to what I did, all of it, even the sins that bear down on me so much as to be crushing. Love calls me to pick up the phone and apologize—not "I'm sorry for what you did to me" or "I'm sorry you felt hurt" but a true confession: *I have not loved you, my neighbor, as myself. I am truly sorry, and I humbly repent.* Love asks me to look around: have I gone wandering down a path that took me away from love? Then I must turn back. Love calls me to make amends: to admit what I have done, and what contributed to it, and what it has done to others.

Love calls me to be wiser—to pay attention, to learn, to ask questions, to assume that my worldview has not yet reached the end of reality. Love shows me I live in community; my experiences do not form the ground of the reality of others. I am responsible for their stories, too: responsible to hear when others speak, to ask when others are silent, and to act when need is expressed. I cannot do this without expanding my mind and opening up to the possibilities of others. Neither can I do it carelessly, lazily, with words and support tossed around without discernment. As much as I am called beyond myself, I am called to a whole community, all of which needs care and compassion.

Love calls me to be kinder—to see the suffering of those around me, to feel my stomach twisted in compassion, to strengthen my hands for service. I am invited into compassionate imagination, where I assume better intent on the part of others than my ego might think is merited. Love asks me to see myself in others. Love, too, asks me to see myself in me: to afford my broken, beat-down, shamed-up self the kindness I am often more eager to offer others. Love asks me to stop telling the story where there is one Perfectly Good Hero and one Irredeemably Evil Monster; the reality, inconveniently, is that as much as I may want to cast myself in one or the other, the narrative arc will not allow such reductionism. Love rejects binaries. Love sees beyond two options. Love witnesses the brokenness in me and the brokenness in others and asks me to see it, too.

Love calls me to be braver. Love calls me to believe enough in love that I do not overexpand to meet the needs of every person nor cut myself down to have no needs of my own. I am invited into risk; love may be constant, but it has a tendency to mess with stability. I am called to trust enough in the protective love of God that I am not afraid to stand up to the brokenness inside me or out. I am asked to speak when the powers that be will seek to silence me. I am challenged to offer my story despite its flaws, its vulnerabilities, its imperfections.

This call to action is not only for me. Love's cry resounds in every corner of the world where the wounded live. Love finds us where we are and invites us not to stay there, urges us onward into better action for ourselves and for the world. Love refuses to let us pretend that we are the center of existence, that those around us are on other journeys to which we have no part; love opens our eyes and minds and hearts to see our shared humanity and its deep needs, in which we might act for the transformation of those who suffer. Love, too, refuses to let us be devoured by the needs and wants of another; love persistently preserves us.

I am convicted by the need for protection and integrity in community. I have known what it is like to lay myself bare in a community, to make my story vulnerable, only to find that others view my vulnerability as a chance for attack. I cannot experience the love of God or know my story or act in love for others if I do so at my own peril. I need community to know who I am and who God calls me to be, but I need a community that will also provide for my safety. No good has been done by further wounding the walking wounded. Love asks me to call communities—family, friends, and especially churches—to account. The church, especially, is burdened with this call. As proclaimers of the good news and servants of the love of God, we are accountable to create a space that protects the vulnerable and invites us into healing.

That healing is not without challenge. Communities that commit themselves fully to the reality of love have the capacity to create a place that reintegrates us. Protected, we can be vulnerable enough to know our stories, brave enough to face our shame. Beloved, we can act in love for others, serving those in need and calling out the powers that seek to destroy. Fully known, we can be called out of brokenness and pain into integrity, into a life knit back together piece by piece. True church is community that loves us into being and transforms us.

I am not foolish enough to think that I know the future of the church, nor powerful enough to have much consequence in it. I only know what I can do in my little corners of the world: my little community church in its elementary-school building where we feed the hungry and sing the songs of God; my little home, with my wife Michelle and the constant stream of pets we love and care for and the children yet to come; my internet work at Queer Grace, where I and other writers bring together the wisdom of the LGBTQ+ Christians who have gone before me and offer it up for those seeking a way in their own wilderness. I live in the paradox that I have worked hard for all of this and yet none of it is a given; all of it is grace. *Every Sunday*, my own pastor Jodi says, *is a miracle. It's a miracle that we are here.* I believe the closer I get to knowing that miracle, the better I know the impossibilities of love.

I have known the impossibilities of love, because I know the stories that testify to it. The disciple Philip was sent from Samaria by the Holy Spirit, called into the wilderness road from Jerusalem to Gaza. There he met a eunuch, an Ethiopian, a powerful man in the queen's court. He was leaving Jerusalem, and in his lap in the chariot was the scroll of the prophet Isaiah. Philip—this lesser-known convert, a Hellenistic Jew with a gentile name, chosen not to preach the word of God but to wait on tables—ran right up to the chariot and asked this powerful black man, "Do you understand what you are reading?" The man replied, "How can I, unless someone guides me?" And so Philip joins the eunuch in his chariot, and together they read Isaiah: *In his humiliation justice was denied him.*

The eunuch asks, "About whom does the prophet say this—himself, or someone else?" And as Philip begins to tell the story of Jesus, I hear also the eunuch's burning question: *Is it me?* Eunuchs were not often born eunuchs nor did they choose it; most had been forcibly castrated by one ruling family or another, so that they might serve the queen or harem without endangering the fidelity of the royal line. They had intentionally been cut off, their chance at their own family and legacy destroyed, in service to empire and wealth. I wonder if the eunuch saw himself in Isaiah, in the man whose life would be taken away from the earth. I wonder if, like me, the eunuch saw in the story of Jesus a man who knew what it was like to be alone.

And so, when the chariot approaches a body of water, the eunuch exclaims, "What is to prevent me from being baptized?" The correct answer is "everything." He is a gentile, a people ethnically and religiously outside the kingdom of God. He is a sexual pariah, both in Greco-Roman culture and in most Jewish practices of the time. He is the rich servant of a foreign political power. All of these should prevent him being baptized. If he has come from Jerusalem, he already knows what he asks is impossible; eunuchs, at the time, would not be permitted to enter the temple, because of what had been done to them.

And Philip gives the correct answer: *nothing*. He climbs from the chariot and into the water (where did the water come from, if this is a desert road?) and fully clothed dunks this powerful Ethiopian eunuch, this impossible convert, this child of God, into the muddy water. The impossibilities of who the eunuch was and how the people of God had been carefully defined were of no interest to the Spirit who had sent Philip into the wilderness.[8]

Impossibilities have been a hallmark all my life. I have accepted being called to serve as a minister in a religion full of people who daily deny my humanity, my goodness, and the worthiness of my love, my vows, and my family. Day by day my inbox adds up with messages from around the world of other queer and trans Christians whose friends, family, and congregations insist that their experience cannot be real—and yet, here we are. The stories of God are not unconcerned with my impossibilities—they are, in fact, dependent on them. What would I have to bring, if all that was in me was unquestioned? What would I receive, if nothing in me was in turmoil?

We are, beloved, the impossibilities of God. We have dared to believe the stories of Scripture. Not the verses easily slung like stones from a condemning hand, but the stories that are real, and make us real, and bring us home. We have faced near-insurmountable boundaries between us and God. We have had the treasured stories of Scripture torn from us by those too bound in fear to see the beauty of our witness. We have been pushed to the edges again and again, our voices silenced, our cries mocked. And every time, the love of God has gone out after us. God has put on callused feet and taken up a knobbly staff to crawl down crevices and call us back to pastures full of lush love, nourishing and sweet. God has taken up a broom and cleared each corner, untucked and retucked each sheet and quilt, turned over pitcher after pitcher to see where we have landed. And God has paced the flagstones of a farm porch, eyes always on the horizon, wondering and waiting, a seat still empty at the table, heaven incomplete until all the family is home.

We have been and are and will be found in such a myriad of ways, but always, always, always love is seeking us.

Dare to be found.

ACKNOWLEDGMENTS

As a child, I treasured the word *independent*. It suggested I was strong and capable and that I needed no one's approval or rescuing. But the truth is, little of my story would exist without the lives that have intersected with mine, the wisdom passed on, the unyielding love that pushed and pulled at me to keep my feet steady and my broken heart bound up and healing. I have needed all of it.

I am grateful to the many public school teachers who guided me along the way, especially Amy Dahlin, who taught me never to be afraid to ask questions of my own knowledge and faith.

I am grateful to the communities that have nurtured me in my faith and call: the youth group at Saint John-in-the-Wilderness, the campus chapel at Saint Olaf College, the children and families of Lutheran Church of Christ the Redeemer, the people of Light of the World and Humble Walk, and now Grace Lutheran Church where I am beyond grateful to serve as pastor. I'm also grateful to all those who modeled an unfearing commitment to the Scriptures and to ministry, whether as pastors in the churches

I attended or as professors in the college and seminary where I begrudgingly accepted the reality of grace.

At this point, there are probably hundreds of people who have taken two minutes to speak encouragement and challenge over me in my years of wrestling. I am especially indebted to Austen for his boundless compassion and companionship, and to Layton for unfailingly answering my panicked messages with tenderness and understanding. And I am unspeakably grateful to the nine women who have helped me feel most found: Ali, Ashley, Gretchen, Hannah, Jamie, Jill, Kim, Michelle, and last but not least Lisa, my friend and now my incredible editor. You have believed in me even before I knew I could.

I remember the many who have gone before me to be seated at the table of the kingdom of heaven: my grandfather and namesake Emiddio Del Giorno; Father Joseph Campbell; Pastor Jennifer Koenig; my uncles Father Maynard Kegler and Vern Gren; and finally, him whose loss is felt the most, my father. Dad, I did my best. I hope you're proud. I know you are.

Mom, you have been many things throughout your life: coach, artist, engineer, teacher, healer. You brought the best of all of it to bear on raising me. Thank you.

My incredible Michelle: at every moment I have been unsure, you have dared me to trust in even half of what you believe I could do. Thank you for every evening you have sacrificed, every dinner you've made, every dog you've shooed out of the room so that I could finish what you challenged me to start. I love you most.

SUGGESTED FURTHER READING

Chapter 1: Real

Family Books

Nelson, Gertrud Mueller. *To Dance with God: Family Ritual and Community Celebration.* New York: Paulist, 1986.

Mangione, Jerre, and Ben Morreale. *La Storia: Five Centuries of the Italian American Experience.* New York: HarperPerennial, 1993.

Treasured Books of Childhood

Wilder, Laura Ingalls. The Little House series. 9 vols. New York: HarperCollins, 2008.

Brink, Carol Ryrie. *Caddie Woodlawn.* New York: Macmillan, 1973.

Tripp, Valerie. *Meet Felicity.* The American Girls Collection. Middleton, WI: Pleasant Company, 1991.

Lowry, Lois. *Number the Stars.* Boston: Houghton Mifflin, 1989.

Lewis, C. S. *The Lion, The Witch, and the Wardrobe.* London: Geoffrey Bles, 1950.

L'Engle, Madeleine. *A Wrinkle in Time.* New York: Farrar, Straus & Giroux, 1962.

Johnston, Johanna. *They Led the Way: 14 American Women.* New York: Scholastic, 1973.

First Religious Books

The Hymnal 1982. New York: Church Hymnal Corp., 1982.

The Book of Common Prayer. New York: Church Hymnal Corp., 1979.

The Good News Bible: Today's English Version. New York: American Bible Society, 1976.

Women of the Bible

Alex, Marlee, Anne de Graaf, and Ben Alex. *Great Men and Women of the Bible.* New York: Paulist, 2001.

Understanding the Four Gospels

Borg, Marcus J. *Meeting Jesus Again for the First Time: The Historical Jesus and the Heart of Contemporary Faith.* San Francisco: HarperOne, 1995.

Powell, Mark Allen. *Fortress Introduction to the Gospels.* Minneapolis: Fortress Press, 1998.

Revelation

Rossing, Barbara R. *The Rapture Exposed: The Message of Hope in the Book of Revelation.* New York: Basic, 2005.

Chapter 2: Good

Matthew Shepard

Kaufman, Moises. *The Laramie Project.* New York: Dramatists Play Service, 2001.

Shepard, Judy, with Jon Barrett. *The Meaning of Matthew: My Son's Murder in Laramie, and a World Transformed.* New York: Plume, 2010.

Chapter 3: Marked

The Courtship Model

Harris, Joshua. *I Kissed Dating Goodbye*. Sisters, OR: Multnomah, 1997.

Anderson, Dianna E. *Damaged Goods: New Perspectives on Christian Purity*. New York: Jericho, 2015. An insightful commentary on the forces that created the courtship model and the purity culture in which it began.

Creation Accounts

Hartke, Austen. *Transforming: The Bible and the Lives of Transgender Christians*. Louisville: Westminster John Knox, 2018.

Contradictions within Literalism

Jacobs, A. J. *The Year of Living Biblically: One Man's Humble Quest to Follow the Bible as Literally as Possible*. New York: Simon & Schuster, 2008.

Evans, Rachel Held. *A Year of Biblical Womanhood: How a Liberated Woman Found Herself Sitting on Her Roof, Covering Her Head, and Calling Her Husband "Master."* Nashville: Thomas Nelson, 2012.

Slavery

Noll, Mark A. *The Civil War as a Theological Crisis*. Chapel Hill: University of North Carolina Press, 2015.

Paul

Loader, William. *Sexuality in the New Testament: Understanding the Key Texts*. Louisville: Westminster John Knox, 2010.

Further Suggested Reading

Brownson, James V. *Bible, Gender, Sexuality: Reframing the Church's Debate on Same-Sex Relationships.* Grand Rapids: Eerdmans, 2013.

Lose, David. *Making Sense of Scripture: Big Questions about the Book of Faith.* Minneapolis: Augsburg Fortress, 2009.

Vines, Matthew. *God and the Gay Christian: The Biblical Case in Support of Same-Sex Relationships.* New York: Convergent Books, 2015.

Chapter 4

Definitions of Sin

Brown, Brené. *The Gifts of Imperfection: Let Go of Who You Think You're Supposed to Be and Embrace Who You Are.* Center City, MN: Hazelden Publishing, 2010.

Jones, Serene. *Feminist Theory and Christian Theology.* Minneapolis: Fortress Press, 2000.

Chapter 5

Reformation and Eucharistic Interpretation

MacCulloch, Diarmaid. *The Reformation: A History.* New York: Penguin, 2005.

Chapter 6

Hermeneutics of Suspicion

Ricoeur, Paul. *Freud and Philosophy: An Essay on Interpretation.* Translated by Denis Savage. New Haven: Yale University Press, 1965.

Schüssler Fiorenza, Elisabeth. *Bread Not Stone: The Challenge of Feminist Biblical Interpretation.* Boston: Beacon, 1995.

Theologies of Trauma

Brock, Rita Nakashima, and Rebecca Ann Parker. *Proverbs of Ashes: Violence, Redemptive Suffering, and the Search for What Saves Us.* Boston: Beacon, 2002.

Cone, James H. *The Cross and the Lynching Tree.* Maryknoll, NY: Orbis, 2013.

Gutiérrez, Gustavo. *A Theology of Liberation: History, Politics, and Salvation.* Maryknoll, NY: Orbis, 1988.

Althaus-Reid, Marcella. *The Queer God.* London: Routledge, 2003.

Winner, Lauren. *Wearing God: Clothing, Laughter, Fire, and Other Overlooked Ways of Meeting God.* San Francisco: HarperOne, 2016. All of her books are excellent, but I have a particular appreciation for this one.

Chapter 7

Erlander, Daniel. *Manna and Mercy: God's Unfolding Promise to Mend the Entire Universe.* Freeland, WA: Daniel Erlander Publications, 1992. I was most significantly awakened to the dichotomy between the Christian cultural images of God and the scriptural images of God through this book.

Chapter 8

On Paul

Harrill, J. Albert. *Paul the Apostle: His Life and Legacy in Their Roman Context.* Cambridge: Cambridge University Press, 2012.

Roetzel, Calvin J. *The Letters of Paul: Conversations in Context.* Louisville: Westminster John Knox, 2015.

Wright, N. T. *Paul: In Fresh Perspective.* Minneapolis: Fortress Press, 2008.

Martin Luther's Paradox

Luther, Martin. *Three Treatises.* Minneapolis: Fortress Press, 1970.

Women in Scripture

Conner, Alice. *Fierce: Women of the Bible and Their Stories of Violence, Mercy, Bravery, Wisdom, Sex, and Salvation.* Minneapolis: Fortress Press, 2017.

Trible, Phyllis. *Texts of Terror: Literary-Feminist Readings of Biblical Narratives.* Philadelphia: Fortress Press, 1984.

Al-Anon and Codependency

Beattie, Melody. *Codependent No More: How to Stop Controlling Others and Start Caring for Yourself.* Center City, MN: Hazelden, 1986.

Blueprint for Progress: Al-Anon's Fourth Step Inventory. Virginia Beach, VA: Al-Anon Family Group Headquarters, 2004.

Courage to Change: One Day at a Time in Al-Anon II. New York: Al-Anon Family Group Headquarters, 1992.

How Al-Anon Works for Families and Friends of Alcoholics. Virginia Beach, VA: Al-Anon Family Group Headquarters, 2008.

Chapter 9

Matthew 5, Forgiveness, and Nonviolent Resistance

Linn, Dennis, Sheila Fabricant Linn, and Matthew Linn. *Don't Forgive Too Soon: Extending the Two Hands That Heal.* New York: Paulist, 1997.

Wink, Walter. *Jesus and Nonviolence: A Third Way.* Minneapolis: Fortress Press, 2003.

Bonhoeffer, Dietrich. *Letters and Papers from Prison.* Minneapolis: Fortress Press, 2015.

Chapter 10

The next thing to read, beloved, is your own story.

NOTES

PROLOGUE: LOST

1. This "lost chapter" is Luke 15:1–32.

CHAPTER 1: REAL

1. Hannah: 1 Samuel 1:1–2:10.
   Mary Magdalene: seven demons exorcised (Luke 8:1–2), following Jesus to the cross (Matthew 27:55–61; Mark 15:40–47; Luke 23:48–56; John 19:25–27), present at the empty tomb (Matthew 28:1–10; Mark 16:1–8; Luke 24:1–10; John 20:1–18).
2. Deborah: Judges 4:1–24.
3. Matthew 1:18–2:23, compared to Luke 1:26–56, 2:1–40.
4. Genesis 1:1–2:4a, compared to Genesis 2:4b–25.
5. Notice, for example, the difference in which women first witnessed the empty tomb alongside Mary Magdalene, in Matthew 28:1–10; Mark 16:1–8; Luke 24:1–10; and John 20:1–18.
6. Babel: Genesis 11:1–9.
   Reed Sea: Exodus 14:1–25.
   Samson: Judges 14–16.
   Elijah: Consider perhaps 2 Kings 2:1–12.
   Psalms: Consider the beast Leviathan of Psalm 104:25–26.
   Song of Solomon: The whole book is beautiful; I suggest reading all of it.

Isaiah: See, for example, the appearance of Leviathan in Isaiah 27:1.

7. Samuel and Kings and Chronicles: Notice, for example, that the writers of the book of 2 Chronicles completely leave out Solomon's foreign wives (2 Chronicles 8–9), while the writers of 1 Kings directly attribute his royal downfall to such wives (1 Kings 11:1–13).

   Daniel: The story of Nebuchadnezzar's demand for worship and the fiery punishment for Shadrach, Meshach, and Abednego (Daniel 3:1–30) bears a lot of resemblance to comedic satire.

   Paul on the road to Damascus: See the narrative in Acts 9:1–19 as compared to Paul's own account of the event in Acts 22:6–16.

8. John 1:1–18.

CHAPTER 2: GOOD

1. Jesus's last meal: Matthew 26:17–30; Mark 14:12–31; Luke 22:7–38; John 13:1–17:26, especially the foot washing in John 13:1–35.

   Jesus in the garden: Matthew 26:36–56; Mark 14:32–52; Luke 22:39–53; John 18:1–11.

2. Matthew 21:1–11; Mark 11:1–10; Luke 19:28–38; John 12:12–19.

3. Matthew 21:12–17; Mark 11:15–19; Luke 19:45–48. See also John 2:14–22, where the cleansing of the temple is disconnected from the passion narrative.

4. Most commonly observed are the challenges with religious leaders (Matthew 21:23–23:39; Mark 11:27–12:44; Luke 20:1–21:4) or the Greeks who "wish to see Jesus" (John 12:20–36).

5. "His blood be on us and on our children!" (Matthew 27:25); note that, in matching accounts in Mark 15:6–15; Luke 23:13–25; and John 18:38b–19:16, this line is absent.

6. Matthew 26:1–16; Mark 14:1–11; Luke 22:1–6. Note that tied up in Matthew's and Mark's accounts of the betrayal is an unnamed woman anointing Jesus with oil (often connected with Mary of Bethany, as in John 12:1–8, but the timelines are different).

7. Jesus, particularly in the Gospel of Mark, often seeks to keep his work hidden. He silences both the humans who experience his miracles (Mark 1:40–45, 5:21–43, 8:22–26) and the demons he exorcises (Mark 1:32–34, 3:7–12). He also orders his disciples, after Peter's confession "You are the Messiah," to tell no one (Matthew 16:13–20; Mark 8:27–30; Luke 9:18–22). This is not consistent; sometimes Jesus clearly wants his work proclaimed (Mark 5:1–20), and similar stories in other Gospels (Matthew 9:18–26, for example, as compared with Mark 5:21–43) do not record the same commands for silence.

8. With the hungry: Matthew 14:13–21; Mark 6:31–44; Luke 9:10–17; John 6:1–14; also Matthew 15:32–39 and Mark 8:1–9.
   With tax collectors: Matthew 9:9–13; Mark 2:13–17; Luke 5:27–32, 18:9–14, 19:1–10.
   With fishermen: Matthew 4:18–22; Luke 5:1–11.
   With the leprous: Matthew 8:1–4; Mark 1:40–45; Luke 5:12–16; also Luke 17:11–19 and many more.
   With demon-possessed: Matthew 8:28–34; Mark 5:1–20; Luke 8:26–39; also Luke 4:31–37, and many more.
   With women in general: Luke 8:1–3.
   With a Samaritan woman: John 4:1–42.
   With an adulteress: John 7:53–8:11.
   With a woman learning at his feet: Luke 10:38–42.
   Kingdom of God at hand: many instances, but specifically Luke 4:16–30.

9. Luke 24:13–24.

10. Matthew 28:1; Mark 16:1; Luke 23:56; also John 19:42–20:1, but the timing is different.

11. Matthew 27:3–10 records Judas's death as suicide; Acts 1:18–19 says that Judas fell and "burst open in the middle." Both stories call the field Judas's money was spent on Hakeldama, Aramaic for *Field of Blood*. Judas, like Saul with David, had "walked alongside" Jesus "in the house of God"—see Psalm 55.

12. The touch of death: Exodus 12:1–32.
    Elijah in his cloak: 1 Kings 19:1–10.
    Babylonian songs: Psalm 137.

13. Simon Peter denies knowing Jesus in Matthew 26:33–35; Mark 14:29–31; Luke 22:33–34; and John 13:36–38.

CHAPTER 3: MARKED

1. Not her real name.
2. Not the church's real name.
3. Not his real name.
4. Genesis 1:1–2:4a and Genesis 2:4b–25, as before.
5. Genesis 19:1–11.
6. Ezekiel 16:49–50.
7. Jude 1:7.
8. Judges 19:1–30.
9. Leviticus 18:22 and 20:13 are the best-known verses; most of the rest of the text, in Christian practice and quotation, is not known or followed.
10. A geocentric (earth at the center) model was the predominant way of understanding the cosmos for thousands of years. It still affects our language today—we describe the sun as rising and setting, despite the scientific fact that it is the earth's rotation on an axis that creates sunrise and sunset. Geocentrism informed the writers of Scripture as well, thus references to the sun's ability to stand still (Joshua 10:12–13; Habakkuk 3:11) and the immovability of the earth (1 Chronicles 16:30; Psalm 93:1, 96:10, 104:5).
11. Ephesians 6:5; Colossians 3:22; 1 Timothy 6:1; Titus 2:9; and 1 Peter 2:18.
12. The "clobber verses" of Paul are found in 1 Corinthians 6:9 and 1 Timothy 1:10, along with Paul's story of wickedness in Romans 1:18–32.

CHAPTER 4: SHAMED

1. Psalm 51:5.
2. The concept of fragmentation (and the traditional definition of sin as "narcissistic self-definition") can be found in Serene Jones,

Feminist Theory and Christian Theology (Minneapolis: Fortress Press, 2000).

3. Matthew 5:27–30; John 7:53–8:11.
4. Often associated with Jesus's teaching in Matthew 16:24–26; Mark 8:34–38; Luke 9:23–27.
5. Matthew 23:1–36; Mark 12:38–40; Luke 20:45–47.
6. Luke 1:46–55.
7. Polygamy was not an uncommon practice in biblical times. Esau had two wives (Genesis 26:34 and 28:6–9). Moses had three wives: Zipporah (Exodus 2:21), the daughter of Hobab (Numbers 10:29), and an Ethiopian woman (Numbers 12:1). Hannah's husband Elkanah had another wife, Peninnah (1 Samuel 1:1–8). David, notably, had seven wives who bore him children: Ahinoam of Jezreel, Abigail of Carmel, Maachah the daughter of King Talmai of Geshur, Haggith, Abital, Eglah, and Bathsheba (1 Chronicles 3:1–9); this list does not include Michal, daughter of King Saul (1 Samuel 18:17–29), likely because she critiqued David's excessive celebration of the return of the ark and died childless (2 Samuel 6:12–23). Solomon had an extreme number of wives—seven hundred princesses and three hundred concubines (1 Kings 11:1–3).

It is notable as well that Paul's letters to Timothy and Titus require that church leaders have only one wife (1 Timothy 3:2, 12; Titus 1:6). There is significant debate as to whether this was a churchwide standard for all believers that Paul was reinforcing, or if this was only a requirement of bishops, deacons, and other overseers of the community.

In addition to polygamy, it was not uncommon for men to take their wives' servants for sexual relations and to bear children, creating slave concubines. Abraham takes Sarah as his wife but also uses her slave-girl Hagar (Genesis 16:1–16), through which Ishmael is conceived. Jacob marries both Leah and Rachel (Genesis 29:1–30), and their slave-girls Bilhah and Zilpah bear children for Jacob (Genesis 30:1–13). These women did not have rights to the children they bore; they were considered the children of their mother's mistress.

Levirate marriage addressed the concerns of a woman whose husband died without giving her a son. To protect her (since women had little chance of making a living without the support of a father, a husband, or a son), the dead husband's brother was required to take her in marriage and give his brother's lineage to the firstborn son of that union (Deuteronomy 25:5–10). Onan, a son of Judah, famously refused to perform this duty and for it was struck down (Genesis 38:1–11); Boaz, before marrying Ruth, spoke to the next-of-kin who should have married her, and received permission from the next-of-kin and the elders to "take the right of redemption" (Ruth 3:6–4:12).

In his first letter to the church at Corinth, Paul suggests that those who are unmarried or widowed "remain unmarried, as I am," but if they could not exercise self-control, they should marry rather than "be aflame with passion" (1 Corinthians 7:6–9).

8. Ruth 1:1–22.
9. His cry of bitterness: Job 6:11. His wife survives: Job 2:9–10.
10. Burning bush: Exodus 3:1–6.
    Mount Sinai: Exodus 19:16–19.
    Pillar of cloud and fire: Exodus 13:21–22.
11. Moses is charged with relaying the message from God to the people. There are moments when Moses expands on or clarifies God's commands—for example, in instituting rest on the Sabbath day, God proclaims it a day of "solemn rest" on which work cannot be done (Exodus 20:8–11, 23:12) under penalty of death (Exodus 31:12–17); Moses adds, "You shall kindle no fire in all your dwellings on the Sabbath day" (Exodus 35:3).
12. Psalm 31:24.

CHAPTER 5: FED

1. "Take, eat; this is my body": Matthew 26:26–30; Mark 14:17–21; Luke 22:14–23.
   ". . . no life in you": John 6:52–59.
2. "in remembrance of me": Luke 22:19; 1 Corinthians 11:25.

3. Freedom from slavery: Exodus 14:1–25.
   Quail and wafers: Exodus 16:1–36.
   Wine at a wedding: John 2:1–11.
   Simon and the sinful woman: Luke 7:36–50.
   Emmaus: Luke 24:1–35.

CHAPTER 6: PINNED

1. Divorce: Women in biblical times, up to and including the time of Jesus and Paul, could not initiate their own divorce. Any divorced women in Scripture have been "put away" by their husbands (see, for example, the Samaritan woman in John 4:1–19, who has "had five husbands"; more correctly, five men have married and divorced her). Moses's teaching had allowed for divorce to be initiated by the husband if "something objectionable" was found about the wife (Deuteronomy 24:1–4). Jesus, notably, revoked this permission (Matthew 5:31–32; also Matthew 19:1–12 and Mark 10:1–12). Divorced women in that time would have little to no chance of providing for themselves. See also "Traditional Biblical Marriage" in the notes for chapter 4.
   Chairs: Leviticus 15:19–24.
2. Acts 10:1–16.
3. Leviticus 11:1–23.
4. Acts 11:1–18.
5. Matthew 23:23.
6. Stealing his brother's birthright: Genesis 25:29–34, 27:1–45.
   Serving Laban: Genesis 29:15–30.
   Making trouble with Laban: Genesis 31:1–21.
   Sending gifts to Esau: Genesis 32:3–5.
   Splitting up for safety: Genesis 32:6–21.
7. Wrestling at Peniel: Genesis 32:22–32.
   Jacob and Esau meet: Genesis 33:1–4.
8. Psalm 6:6.
9. Phyllis Trible, "Wrestling with Faith," *Biblical Archaeology Review* 40, no. 5 (September/October 2014).

CHAPTER 7: SHUT UP

1. Jeremiah 20:9.
2. At creation: Genesis 1:1–2, 1:9–10.
   Hearing Joseph: Genesis 37–50, and particularly 45:8.
   Sending plagues: Exodus 7:14–11:10.
   Dry land: Exodus 14:15–22.
3. "Stay free": A summary of the law given in the books of Exodus through Deuteronomy.
   Nathan the prophet: 2 Samuel 11:27b–12:15.
   Psalmist: Psalm 139: "If I make my bed in Sheol, you are there . . . even the darkness is not dark to you."
4. Desert flame: Exodus 3:1–15.
   Deborah's palm tree: Judges 4:1–5.
   Mordecai: Esther 4:13–14.
5. The voices of the prophets: Many, but particularly Isaiah 1:17, 10:1–2, 58:6–11, 61:1; Jeremiah 5:28, 7:6, 22:3; Ezekiel 16:49, 18:12–13, 22:29; Amos 4:1–2; Zechariah 7:9–10; and Malachi 3:5.
   The servant of God: Isaiah 42:1–4.
6. In a dove: Matthew 3:13–17; Mark 1:9–11; Luke 3:21–22.
   Kissed: Matthew 26:47–50; Mark 14:43–46; Luke 22:47–53.
   God's death: Matthew 27:45–51; Mark 15:33–38; Luke 23:44–46.
   Borrowed tomb: Joseph of Arimathea is wealthy enough to get the body and have it buried; Matthew 27:57–60; Mark 15:42–46; Luke 23:50–54; John 19:38–42.
7. Walking through walls: Luke 24:36; John 20:19.
   Cooking fish: John 21:9–13.
   Wrists and feet: Luke 24:39–40; John 20:20–29.
8. "Yes": Luke 1:38: "Let it be with me according to your word."
9. Genesis 1:26–31.
10. Ha'adam without a partner: Genesis 2:18–25; most translations render "Ha'adam" as "the man" in these verses, but the Hebrew word for *man* (ish) does not appear in the text until after woman (ishah) appears.
11. Genesis 16:1–14.

12. His mother puts him in, Miriam watches him, and the daughter of Pharaoh draws him out. Exodus 2:1–10.
13. Rahab: Joshua 2:1–21, 6:15–25; she may also be the Rahab of the ancestors of Jesus in Matthew 1:5.
    Ruth: Ruth 1–4; she is named in the line of Jesus in Matthew 1:5.
14. Mary: Luke 1:34–35.
    Ministry support for Jesus: Luke 8:1–3, 10:38–42.
    At the cross: Matthew 27:55–61; Mark 15:40–47; Luke 23:48–56; John 19:25–27.
    At the tomb: Matthew 28:1–10; Mark 16:1–8; Luke 24:1–10; John 20:1–18.
    An idle tale: Luke 24:10–11.
15. Acts 2:1–4.
16. A mighty arm: Exodus 6:2–8.
    God's footstool: Isaiah 66:1.
    Like an eagle: Deuteronomy 32:11–12.
    In the shadow of your wings: Psalm 17:8, 63:7, 91:4.
    As a hen gathers her chicks: Matthew 23:37–39; Luke 13:31–35.
17. "You are my child": Exodus 4:22; Psalm 2:7; Hosea 11:1.
    "You are beloved": Matthew 3:17; Mark 1:11; Luke 3:22.
    "I am with you always": Matthew 28:20.
18. Lamentations 3:22–23.
19. Isaiah 43:1–4.
20. Isaiah 49:14–15.
21. Isaiah 42:13–14.
22. John 11:17–44.
23. The Father's house: Luke 2:41–51; also John 14:1–3.
    Love in the face of hate: Matthew 5:43–48; Luke 6:27–36.
    Hiding revelation: Matthew 11:25–30; Luke 10:21–24.
24. Hallowed name: Matthew 6:9; Luke 11:2.
    Kingdom to come: Matthew 6:10; Luke 11:2.
    Feeding and protecting: Matthew 6:11; Luke 11:3.
    Suffering: Matthew 6:13; Luke 11:4; Matthew 26:36–46; Mark 13:32–42; Luke 22:39–46.
    "Father, forgive them": Luke 23:34.
25. Luke 15:1–32.

1. 1 Corinthians 11:23–25.
2. See again the explanation of levirate marriage in the notes on chapter 4.
   Ruth: Ruth 4:1–21.
   Abigail: 1 Samuel 25:2–42.
   Proverbs 31: Specifically verses 10–31.
   Divorced women: See the explanation of biblical heterosexuality in the notes for chapter 6.
   Widowed women: Mark 12:41–44; Luke 21:1–4.
   Hemorrhaging women: Matthew 9:18–26; Mark 5:21–43; Luke 8:40–56.
3. 1 Corinthians 14:26–36.
4. Prisca and Aquila: Acts 18:1–4 ("Aquila and Priscilla"), 18:18 ("Priscilla and Aquila"), 18:24–28 ("Aquila and Priscilla"); Romans 16:3 ("Priscilla and Aquila"); 1 Corinthians 16:19 ("Aquila and Priscilla"); 2 Timothy 4:19 ("Prisca and Aquila"). Phoebe: Romans 16:1–2.
5. *malakoi* and *arsenokoitai*: found in 1 Corinthians 6:9, and *arsenokoitai* also in 1 Timothy 1:10. *arsenokoitai* is a combination of the Greek words *arsen* (male) and *koite* (a bed), so it is often translated "homosexual" or "sodomite."

   porneia: Along with *pornos*, this is a Greek word connected to some type of culturally defined sexual immorality; it is the root word of *pornography* and has some connotations with sex work or other economic or social requirements for sexual relations. *Pornos* is the person who participates in the act, *porneia* is the act itself; both words are used much more than *malakoi* or *arsenokoitai* and apply to all genders. *Porneia* is usually translated *fornication* or *sexual immorality*. Paul condemns *pornoi* (the plural of *pornos*) in 1 Corinthians 5:9–11, along with 1 Corinthians 6:9; Ephesians 5:5; and 1 Timothy 1:10; and they are also found in lists of the condemned in Hebrews 12:16, 13:4; Revelation 21:8, 22:15.

   Porneia appears in several other places in the New Testament. Jesus permits divorce on grounds of *porneias*, usually translated *adultery* or *infidelity* (Matthew 5:32, 19:9); it is also in his list of evil things that come out of the heart (Matthew 15:19; Mark 7:21). Jesus's followers who have turned against him say that they are not children of *porneias*, "not illegitimate." When the gentiles are welcomed into the Christian community without circumcision, they do have to keep to certain laws, specifically "from what has been polluted by idols, from *porneias*, from anything strangled, and from blood" (Acts 15:20, 15:29, 21:25). Paul also names and condemns *porneia* in 1 Corinthians 5:1, 6:13, 6:18, 7:2; 2 Corinthians 12:21; Galatians 5:19; Ephesians 5:3; Colossians 3:5; and 1 Thessalonians 4:3.

atimia: disgrace or dishonor. This is the adjective in Romans 1:26 that describes the passions into which the idolaters were given, and there is often translated *degrading* or *vile*. As a noun, Paul also uses it throughout his letters. Sometimes it is translated as *common* or *ordinary* (as the nonspecial use of pottery in Romans 9:21 and 2 Timothy 2:20). Sometimes it is used in parallel with *honor* (*timia*) as a contrast or to suggest a wide spectrum (1 Corinthians 15:43; 2 Corinthians 6:8). When Paul rejects men with long hair, he calls it *atimia*, sometimes translated *degrading* or *a dishonor*.

6. Watching a stoning: Acts 7:54–8:1.
Wrathful: Acts 9:1–2, recounted again in Acts 22:4–6 and Acts 26:9–11.
Trained in scriptural interpretation: Acts 22:3, 26:4–7; Galatians 1:14; Philippians 3:4–6.
Knocked down: Acts 9:3–9, recounted again in Acts 22:6–11 and Acts 26:12–18.
Changing: Acts 9:20–21, recounted again in Acts 22:17–21 and Acts 26:19–20.
Explanations: Most of his speeches in Acts and his letters.
Horrified: Galatians 1:6–9, 3:1–5, 5:2–12.
Wrong opinions: See above notes re: slavery, women.
7. Isaiah 30:12–13; my translation is based on Isaiah 30:12–21.
8. Paul encounters an altar "to an unknown God" in Athens and uses it as a launch point for his explanation about Jesus (Acts 17:16–34).

9. Paul in Troas: Acts 20:7–12.
   Headed toward Jerusalem: Acts 20:22–24.
10. 1 Thessalonians 4:13–18.
11. See Paul's insistence on inclusion at the Lord's Supper in 1 Corinthians 10:14–17 and 1 Corinthians 11:17–34.
12. Galatians 1:6, 3:2, 5:14.
13. Based on Romans 8:38–39.

CHAPTER 9: WIDE

1. The refining fire: one potential understanding of the experience of purification, based on images of God as a refining fire, either in this life (Job 23:10; Psalm 66:10; Proverbs 17:3; Isaiah 1:25, 48:10; Jeremiah 9:7; Zechariah 13:9) or in the time of judgment (Malachi 3:3) or resurrection (1 Corinthians 3:13; 1 Peter 1:7) that is to come.
2. Hebrew midwives: Exodus 1:15–21.
   Moses's mouth: Exodus 4:10–17.
   The violence of Egypt: The freed slaves quickly turn to greed (Exodus 16:19–20) and idolatry (Exodus 32:1–6).
   Prophets and preachers: All of them, but specifically here Elijah (1 Kings 18:20–40).
3. The Beatitudes of Matthew 5:1–12 and Luke 6:20–23.
4. Turning the other cheek: Matthew 5:38–48 and Luke 6:27–31.
5. Matthew 25:1–13.
6. Seventy times seven: Matthew 18:21–22 and Luke 17:5–6.
   Rebuke: Matthew 18:15–20.
   Little ones lost: Matthew 18:10–14.
7. Exodus 16:13–21; Matthew 14:13–21; Revelation 22:17.

CHAPTER 10: FOUND

1. 1 Samuel 2:1–1 and Luke 1:46–48.
2. Luke 15:10.
3. Matthew 11:28–30.
4. "Darkness is not dark": Psalm 139:12.

"Little girl, get up": Mark 5:41.

"Your faith has made you well": Matthew 9:22; Mark 5:34; and Luke 8:48.

5. Bush: Exodus 3:1–6.

Flame: Exodus 13:21–22; Acts 2:1–4.

Silence: 1 Kings 19:12–13.

Split skies: Matthew 3:13–17; Mark 1:9–11; Luke 3:21–22.

Broken bread: Luke 24:13–35; Jesus the bread of life in John 6:35.

6. Unclean: Acts 10:1–16.

Foreign wives and children: The histories of Ezra and Nehemiah tell the story of casting out foreign wives and children from the people of God (Ezra 9:1–10:44; Nehemiah 13:23–27). Many scholars think the book of Ruth was also written down at or near this time, as a rejection of this decision.

7. Gleaning: Leviticus 19:9–10, 23:22.

Sacrifices: Leviticus 14:21–22.

8. Philip's background is found in Acts 6:1–6 and Acts 8:4–13; the eunuch's story is found in Acts 8:26–40.